What is Power?

Byung-Chul Han

What is Power?

Translated by Daniel Steuer

polity

First published in German as *Was ist Macht?* © Philipp Reclam jun. GmbH & Co. KG, Stuttgart, 2005

Polity Press
65 Bridge Street
Cambridge CB2 1UR, UK

Polity Press
101 Station Landing
Suite 300
Medford, MA 02155, USA

ISBN-13: 978-1-5095-1609-4
ISBN-13: 978-1-5095-1610-0 (pb)

A catalogue record for this book is available from the British Library.

Typeset in 10.75 on 14 Janson Text by
Servis Filmsetting Ltd, Stockport, Cheshire
Printed and bound in Clays Ltd, Popson Street, Bungay

The publisher has used its best endeavours to ensure that the URLs for external websites referred to in this book are correct and active at the time of going to press. However, the publisher has no responsibility for the websites and can make no guarantee that a site will remain live or that the content is or will remain appropriate.

Every effort has been made to trace all copyright holders, but if any have been inadvertently overlooked the publisher will be pleased to include any necessary credits in any subsequent reprint or edition.

For further information on Polity, visit our website: politybooks.com

CONTENTS

PREFACE

When it comes to the concept of power, theoretical chaos still reigns. While the existence of the phenomenon itself cannot be doubted, the concept remains altogether ambiguous. For some, it means repression; for others, it is a constructive element in communication. Legal, political and sociological notions of power remain unreconciled. Power is sometimes associated with freedom, sometimes with coercion. For some power is based on common action, for others on struggle. Some draw a sharp line between power and violence. For others, violence is just a more extreme form of power. At one moment power is associated with the law, at another with arbitrariness.

Given this theoretical confusion, we shall look for a flexible concept of power that is able to unite these divergent ideas. Thus, the task is to formulate a basic form of power from which we can, by modifying its inner structural elements, derive the different forms in which power may appear. This is the theoretical approach the book pursues, and the book aims, in this way, to deprive power of that power it has on account of the fact that we do not fully understand what it actually is.[1]

1

The Logic of Power

Power is usually defined as a causal relation: the power of the *ego* is the cause which effects a particular behaviour in an *alter* against the latter's will. It enables the *ego* to impose *his or her* decisions without having to show any consideration for the *alter*. Thus, the *ego*'s power limits the *alter*'s freedom. The *alter* suffers the will of the *ego* as something alien. This common idea of power does not do justice to its complexity. Processes of power are not exhausted by attempts to break resistance or to compel obedience. Power does not have to take the form of coercion. The fact that there is a will forming that opposes the holder of power actually bears witness to the weakness of that power. The more powerful power is, the more *silent* is its efficacy. Where it needs to draw special attention to itself, it is already weakened.[1]

Neither does power consist in 'neutralizing the will'.[2] The claim here is that the existing power imbalance impedes the formation of a will on the side of the subordinated party, for this party will in any case have to succumb to the will of the holder of power. Hence, the holder of power directs the subordinated party regarding the latter's choices of action. But there are forms of power that exceed such a 'neutralization of the will'. It is the sign of a superior power that those subjected to it explicitly *want* what the holder of power wants, that those subjected to power follow the will of its holder *as if it were their own*, or even *anticipate* that will. The one who is subjected to power may glorify what he or she would have, *in any event*, wanted to do, by declaring it to be in accordance with the will of the superior power, and executing it with a 'Yes!', an emphatic affirmation of that power. Thus, one and the same action takes on a different form in the medium of power because the action of the holder of power is affirmed or internalized by the one subjected to power as his or her *own* action. Power is thus a *phenomenon pertaining to form*. *How* an action is motivated is crucial. Not 'I have to anyhow' but 'I want to' expresses the presence of a superior power. Not the inner 'No', but the emphatic 'Yes!' is the response to a superior power.[3] Causality does not allow for an adequate description of it, because in this case power does not operate like a mechanical push that simply moves a body out of its original trajectory. Rather, its effect is like that of a field in which the body moves *out of its own accord*, so to speak.

The model of coercion does not do justice to the complexity of power. Power as coercion consists in enforcing one's own decisions *against* the will of the other. It therefore displays only a very low degree of mediation between *ego* and *alter*, which relate antagonistically to each other. The *ego* is not received in the *soul of the alter*. The form of power which does not exercise its effects *against* the intended actions of the other but *from within* these contains more mediation. For a superior power is one that forms the future of the other, not one that blocks it. Instead of proceeding against a particular action of the *alter*, it influences or works on the environment of the *alter*'s actions even before they take place, so that the *alter voluntarily* decides in favour of the *ego*'s will, even without the threat of any sanctions. Without the use of any violence [Gewaltausübung],[4] the holder of power takes his place in the *soul* of the other.

The causal model is incapable of describing complex relations. Even organic life as such cannot be understood in terms of causal relations. As opposed to a lifeless and passive thing, an organism does not allow an external cause to have an effect on it without the organism contributing to it. Rather, it reacts *independently* to the cause. This capacity to give an independent response to an external trigger is characteristic of the organic. A lifeless thing, by contrast, does not *respond*. The specificity of life is that it cuts short the external cause, transforms it and lets it begin something new in itself. Life may be dependent on food, but food is not the cause of life. If we can talk of a cause at all in this context, then it is life itself which has the *power* to *turn* what is external to it *into* a cause of specific organic processes.[5] These processes are therefore not simple repetitions of the external cause on the inside. Rather, they are independent achievements, independent decisions of life. It reacts independently to the outside. An external cause is but one of many possible triggers that life itself turns into a cause. Life never just passively suffers such causes. An external cause never achieves an effect without a contribution or decision of the inner. There is no immediate continuation of the outer into the inner, as in the case of the transmission of kinetic energy from one body to another. The category of causality is even less suitable for a description of *mental* life. The complexity of mental life determines the complexity of power processes which cannot be translated into linear relations between cause and effect. This complexity distinguishes power from physical violence, where a simple causality between force, or strength, and effect can be given. This reduction in complexity probably constitutes the advantage of physical violence.

The complex processes of power cannot be adequately described with simple arithmetic. A slight countervailing power may inflict severe damage on a power of superior strength. This affords even a weak opponent great importance, and thus power. Specific political constellations may also give a lot of power to weak parties or nations. And complex interdependencies mean that there is reciprocity of power. If the *ego* needs the cooperation of the *alter*, a dependence of *ego* on *alter* is the result. The *ego* can no longer formulate and enforce his or her demands without taking the *alter* into consideration, because the *alter* has the option of reacting to the *ego*'s attempts at compelling him or her by ending his or her cooperation, which would also put the *ego* into a difficult situation. Thus, the *ego*'s dependence on the *alter* can be perceived and used by the latter as a source of power. Even the very weakest can turn their powerlessness into power by making skilful use of cultural norms.

Furthermore, there is the multifarious dialectic of power to consider. The hierarchical model of power, according to which power simply moves from top to bottom, is undialectical. The more power someone holds, the more he or she is dependent on the advice and cooperation of subordinates. The holder of power may be able to give orders across a vast range of matters. But due to the increasing complexity of such operations, the power in fact passes on to the advisors who tell the holder of power what orders to give. The numerous dependencies of the holder of power become a source of power for the subordinates. They lead to a structural *dispersal of power*.

There is an obstinate belief that power excludes freedom. But this is not the case. The power of the *ego* reaches its peak precisely at the point at which the *alter* voluntarily follows the will of the *ego*. The *ego* does not impose him- or herself on the *alter*. *Free power* is not an oxymoron. It says: the *alter* follows the *ego* out of freedom. Whoever wants to achieve absolute power will have to make *use* not of violence but of the freedom of the other. Absolute power is achieved at the point at which freedom and submission coincide completely.

However, power based on giving orders and power based on freedom and what is taken for granted are not two opposed models. They differ only in *appearance*. Raised to an abstract level, they reveal their common structure. Power allows the *ego to be with him- or herself in the other*. It creates a *continuity of the self*. The *ego* turns *his or her* decisions into reality in the *alter*. Thus, the *ego* is continued in the *alter*. Power creates *spaces* for the *ego* that are *proper* to the *ego*, spaces in which the *ego* can be *with him- or herself* despite the presence of the other. It enables the holder of power to return to *him- or herself* in the other. This continuity can be achieved through the use of coercion as well as through the use of freedom. In the case of obedience out of free choice, the continuity of the *ego* is a very stable one. It is *mediated* with the *alter*. The continuity of self in the case of coercion, by contrast, is fragile due to the absence of mediation. But in *both* cases, power allows the *ego* to continue his or her existence in the *alter*, to be with him- or herself in *alter*. Where mediation is reduced to nil, power turns into violence. Pure violence puts the *alter* in a position of extreme passivity and lack of freedom. There is no longer any *inner* continuity between the *ego* and the *alter*. It is not possible to exert power, in the proper sense, on a passive thing. Thus, violence and freedom are the two end points on the scale of power. The increasing intensity of mediation generates more freedom, or more *feeling* of freedom. The *form* in which power *appears* is therefore conditioned by its inner structure of mediation.

Power is a phenomenon of continuum. It provides the

holder of power with a vast *space of self*. This logic of power explains why the total loss of power is experienced as an absolute *loss of space*. The body of the holder of power, which filled a whole world, so to speak, shrinks to become a shabby piece of meat. The king not only has a natural body, which is mortal, but also a politico-theological body which is co-extensive with his empire. In the case of the loss of his power, he is thrown back onto his small, mortal body.[6] Thus, the loss of power is experienced as a kind of death.

It is erroneous to believe that all power does is inhibit or destroy. Only by looking at it as a medium of communication can we see that it guarantees the swift *flow* of communication in a particular direction. The one subjected to power is brought to (but not necessarily forced to) appropriate the decision of, i.e. the course of action selected by, the holder of power. Power is the 'opportunity to increase the probability of realizing improbable selection combinations'.[7] It steers communication in a specific direction by removing possible discrepancies regarding the selection of actions between the holder of power and the one subjected to power. Thus, it performs the 'transmission of action selection from one point of decision-making to others' in order to 'limit the indefinite complexity of human possibilities to act'.[8] The communicative *lead* of power is not necessarily repressive. Power does not *rest* on repression. Rather, as a means of communication its effects are constructive. Thus, Luhmann defines power as a 'catalyst'. Catalysts accelerate the occurrence of events or influence the development of particular processes without themselves undergoing any change. In this way they produce a 'gain of time' – another way in which the effects of power are *productive*.

Luhmann limits power to those communicative constellations in which a 'no' from those subjected to power is a live possibility. The need for power as a communicative medium emerges in the face of a likely rejection of the selected course of action, i.e. in the case of a communicative bottleneck.[9] The task of power is to transform the always possible 'no' into a 'yes'. As opposed to the negative conception of a power that always says 'no', the function of power as a medium of communication consists in raising the likelihood of 'yes'. The 'yes' of those subjected to power does not need to be jubilatory. But neither is it necessarily the result of coercion. The positivity or productivity of power as 'opportunity' stretches across the *broad space between jubilation and coercion*. The impression of power as destructive or inhibiting results from the fact that only in cases of coercive constellations, which are poor in mediation, is our attention drawn in particular towards power as a striking phenomenon. By contrast, where power does not appear as coercion, it is rarely taken notice of as power, if it is noticed at all. It slips into oblivion behind acceptance, so to speak. Thus, the negative judgement on power is the result of *selective perception*.

Max Weber defines power as follows: '"Power" (Macht) is the probability that one actor within a social relationship will be in a position to carry out his own will despite resistance, regardless of the basis on which this probability rests.'[10] He then goes on to remark that the concept of 'power' is 'sociologically amorphous'. The concept of 'domination', which guarantees 'that a command will be obeyed', by contrast, he sees as 'more precise'. This evaluation is not without its problems. Power is certainly not 'sociologically amorphous'. This impression results from perceiving power from a limited perspective. A more differentiated world produces indirect and less obvious foundations for power, with subtle effects. Their complexity and indirectness lead to the impression that the effects of power are 'amorphous'. As opposed to domination by orders, power does not appear openly. The power of power consists precisely in its capacity to influence decisions and actions without the use of explicit 'orders'.

Power is not opposed to freedom. It is precisely freedom that distinguishes power from violence or coercion. Luhmann, too, ties power to a particular form of 'social relation', one 'in which *both sides could act differently*'.[11] It follows from this that in the case of acting under coercion, no power will form. Even obedience presupposes a degree of freedom as it still rests on a choice. Physical violence, by contrast, also eradicates the possibility of obeying. It is passively *endured*. Obedience possesses more activity and freedom than the passive enduring of violence. It always takes place against a background of an alternative way of acting. The holder of power must also be free. If he were to feel compelled by a situation to make a particular decision, then he would not possess the power – if anything, the compelling situation would. He would be passively at the mercy of the situation. The holder of power must be free in order to *choose* a specific behaviour and impose it. He must at least act under the illusion that the choice is his, under the illusion that he is *free*.

In every act of communication it is in principle open whether the *ego*'s decision is accepted or rejected by the *alter*. However, the power of the *ego* makes it more likely that the *alter* will abide by the decisions taken by the *ego*. Thus, Luhmann understands power as a medium of communication which raises the likelihood that the *alter* will accept the decision of the *ego*. Although this model of power connects power with the idea of freedom, it ties the power relation categorically to the avoidance of a situation that is seen as negative. An example presented by Luhmann makes this clear:

A threatens B with a physical fight which both evaluate negatively. His power consists in the fact that he evaluates a fight less negatively than B, and in the fact that for both sides there is a second, less negative combination of alternatives, which both may choose. In such situations, the greater probability of being able to decide what will happen lies with the one whose constellation of alternatives is the more flexible, so that he can still accept situations which the other already considers too unpleasant.[12]

Thus, Luhmann ties power to a sanction (e.g. being made redundant or being threatened with other disadvantages). In order to exert power, the *ego* must be able to put the *alter* under pressure by means of a sanction. This sanction is a possible course of action that *both* sides, the *ego* and the *alter*, want to avoid – but the *alter* more so than the *ego*. If, for instance, making the *alter* redundant would hurt the *ego* more than the *alter*, the *ego* could not use it as an instrument of power. In this case, redundancy would become a source of power for the *alter*. In Luhmann's words:

A negative sanction is only an alternative that stands at the ready – an alternative that in the normal case, and that is the one on which power is based, *both* sides would rather avoid than put into practice. Power, then, is the result of the fact that the holder of power would find it easier to put up with the execution of the sanction than the one subjected to power. The possibility of imposing sanctions provides power precisely when it is not, and as long as it is not, used. Power therefore ends where it is possible to provoke it. The execution of physical violence is not an application of power, but an expression of its failure...[13]

There are a number of problems with Luhmann's theory of power. To begin with, it is not absolutely necessary for there to be power processes in which *both* sides want to avoid sanctions. If, for instance, the one who holds the power is able to replace *without difficulty* the one who is subordinate, then he or she does not need to shy away from putting the sanction into practice, i.e. sacking the subordinate person. Thus, in order for a power relation to form it need not be the case that there is a possibility whose realization *both* sides want to avoid. It is enough that only one of the sides wants to avoid it. This asymmetry does not necessarily reduce the power of the one in the powerful position. It may even add to that power. More power, in this case, means more freedom for the holder of power, who is free because the other person no longer represents a limit to his or her actions.

Looking at the matter more closely, a power relation does not even require a one-sided desire to avoid a particular possibility, i.e. a desire on the part of the subordinate person. The *alter*'s acceptance of the *ego*'s decision does not need to rest on a fear in the face of a sanction. The *alter*'s 'yes' may affirm the *ego*'s decision without there being any *oblique consideration* of the possibility to be avoided. The power of the *ego* reaches its peak in this sort of emphatic 'yes' on the part of the *alter*, a response that does not contain a trace of a 'yes, alright then'. For Luhmann, by contrast, the exercise of power always depends on a 'yes, alright then'. Yet a truly powerful holder of power does not simply elicit agreement, but enthusiasm and excitement.

According to Luhmann, power increases proportionately with the number of alternative courses for action:

> The power of the power-holder is greater if he can choose from more and more diverse types of decisions for the implementation of power, and it is greater if he can do this in opposition to a partner who himself has more and more diverse alternatives. Power increases with freedom on *both* sides, and, for example, in any given society, in proportion to the alternatives that society creates.[14]

It is certainly a sign of freedom and power that there are numerous possible ways in which the *ego* may act in order to communicate power. And it is also a sign of the *ego*'s power that the *alter* follows the selection made by the *ego* despite attractive alternatives being readily available to him or her. But the freedom that the *alter* enjoys through this broad space of possible actions does not necessarily increase the power of the *ego*. It may even be destabilizing. The *feeling of freedom* on the side of the one who is subordinated to power does not depend on the number of alternatives at his or her disposal. Rather, what is decisive is the structure or intensity of the 'yes' with which the *alter* affirms the *ego*. The emphatic nature of this 'yes', which generates a feeling of freedom, is independent of the number of alternatives for action.

Luhmann assumes that 'the power of the superior over his subordinates and that of the subordinates over their superior can be increased simultaneously by intensifying their relation'.[15] In this, he draws on an approach from management studies that breaks with the hierarchical model of influence: 'The heads of very productive sections have a better leadership system than those of less productive sections. This superior system secures more influence for the head by also offering the subordinates more possibilities for exerting influence.'[16] If a decision is not fully accepted by the subordinates, the superior loses a lot of influence because the influence on decision-making does not coincide with the influence on what is *actually* put into practice by the subordinates. It is perfectly possible that a superior who decides in an authoritarian fashion only has little influence on what actually happens. This, however, does not mean that the subordinates' capacity to take influence would guarantee more influence – not to mention more power – for the superior. An attempt by the superior to enforce his or her decision by threatening the subordinates with redundancies or other sanctions will certainly not increase his power, as this creates a power relation that is based on little mediation and is hence volatile.

11

The superior would gain more in terms of power if the subordinates supported his or her decision. But the superior's power does not increase because the subordinates exercise more influence on him. The intensification of the mutual influencing may increase the *efficiency* of the business, but it does not increase the *power* of the actors. Thus, the decentralization of power may lead to more productivity. And the relations do not become more intense simply because there is more mutual influencing. An intensification of relations is rather achieved through mutual trust or mutual respect. And trust reduces complexity, which has a positive effect on decision processes. Productivity is increased in a communicative atmosphere of trust and respect, which is not, however, identical with an atmosphere of power. The intensification of relations does not simply increase the amount of power. Luhmann's thesis that the power of the superior and that of the subordinates is simultaneously increased by intense relations between them is therefore not convincing.

Power cannot be equated with influence either. Influence can be neutral with respect to power. The intentionality that is typical of power – the one that forms a continuum of the self – is not intrinsic to it. A subordinate who, because of his or her expertise, has a lot of influence on the decision-making process is not therefore necessarily powerful. The capacity to take influence does not automatically lead to a power relation. It must first be *transformed* into one.

On physical violence, Luhmann writes: 'The formation of power stands in an ambivalent relation to physical violence. It exercises violence in the subjunctive, so to speak, i.e. under the condition that it is not actually applied. Violence becomes virtual and is stabilized as a negative possibility.'[17] Although the law-governed state possesses the option of using violence, which is activated in cases of a breach of law, this does not mean that such a state is *based* on violence or any other negative sanction. The sideways glance at the possibility of sanctions being applied, or at the possible use of violence, is not a positive *condition* for the processes of power. Crime is avoided above all because of *respect for the law* rather than the fear of punishment; i.e. it is avoided because the law is my will, my own doing and my freedom. Of course, behind the law there stands the right of the sword.[18] But the law does not *rest* on it. And whoever is only capable of imposing his or her decisions by virtue of the possibility of sanctions possesses little power. The fact that an organization has only very few forms of sanction at its disposal does not say anything about the amount of power it actually has. From the point of view of the *logic of power*, it is perfectly conceivable that there might be a powerful organization that does not have a single sanction at its disposal. As he ties power to the possibility of sanctions, Luhmann loses the sense that there could be a *free power*.

Increasing complexity in an organization can also lead to a complete separation of the organization from the individuals who act in it. In that case, it becomes an independent, anonymous entity.[19] In Kafka's works, we find telling pictures of this process, a process which involves the alienation of acting individuals from their actions. Thus, Luhmann's remarks on modern organization sound truly Kafkaesque:

[T]he logic of the organization requires and enforces the weirdest things: as a worker, you have to drill the same holes hour after hour; as a patient, you have to wake up at six in the morning and take your temperature, despite the fact that you are ill; as a professor, you must take the minutes of meetings that are almost always irrelevant and without consequence. With the help of this mechanism – organization – the most surprising selection of actions can be achieved. The range and variety of these actions is far greater than could be motivated by the use of force.[20]

13

The rigidity of the organizational structure produces certain compulsions [*Zwänge*]. But Luhmann confuses these compulsions with power. He writes: 'No tyrant of the past, no allegedly absolute ruler of historical empires was ever able to form a concentration of power reaching such dimensions, if we take the number and diversity of the decisions that are determined for the actors as a measure. Not even terror is an equal to organization.'[21] What is problematic is that, in this passage, Luhmann understands the increase in decisions taken for others as an increase in power, while in other places he assumes a positive relationship between power and freedom. Recall that he said that '[p]ower increases with freedom on both sides, and, for example, in any given society, in proportion to the alternatives that society creates'. For Luhmann, power depends on decisions and the imposition of selection patterns. The more complex an organization becomes, the more power it needs, i.e. the more selections it must perform. This thesis is questionable in so far as selections are not exclusively made on the basis of power. Power does not increase in direct proportion to the amount of decisions made.

In light of the communicative structure of modern organizations, Luhmann draws the following conclusion: 'Notwithstanding all this, there are many indications that power mechanisms are among the losers in the competition between the factors of social evolution.'[22] According to Luhmann, power does not possess the necessary complexity for modern societies because it 'operates at a much too concrete level'. Modern forms of organization, he says, cannot be pushed through 'the bottleneck of action selections that can be mutually anticipated'.[23] Luhmann's evaluation that power belongs to the factors that will lose out in the course of social evolution results from his approach to the theory of power, which limits power to the action selection that takes place in the interactions between human beings. Power is the 'power held by individuals over other individuals'.[24]

Luhmann is well aware that the exercise of power in the form of a 'selection process' is 'dependent on systemic structures'. The system generates a *particular* constellation of possible actions within which power-guided communication takes place. Thus, power is a '*structure-dependent selection*'. The various possible constellations among which the selection process takes place are determined by the system. The actors in power-guided communication are embedded in a situation that is generated by the system, a situation which *prefigures* the interpersonal power relations in each case. This prefiguration may also happen *pre-consciously*. But Luhmann remains unaware of the possibility of a *pre-reflective* prefiguration, not least because, according to his theory of power, power-guided communication takes place exclusively in the form of a transparent and *conscious* action selection. There is no place in his theory for the form of power that is inscribed in the continuum between the *ego* and the *alter before* either of them has made any conscious selection.

Since Luhmann thinks of power mainly as located in *linear* communicative relations between individual actors, he does not really notice the *spatial* power which appears in the form of a continuum, a totality. A space may influence lines of communication without even being noticed by those communicating through these lines. Often what is *absent* has more power than what is present. Spatial power may also manifest itself in the manner of *gravitation*, establishing an overall order by arranging dispersed forces into a form. Its effects cannot then be described in terms of linear causality. Power, in these instances, does not act as a cause which effects a particular action carried out by the one subjugated to power. Rather, it opens up a *space* which gives an action a direction, i.e. a *sense*. Such a *space* precedes *linear* causality or linear chains

15

of action. It is a *domain* within which one person may have more power, i.e. may be more *dominant*, than another. Power founds a location that precedes *individual* power relations.

Power constitutes different kinds of continuity. We already pointed out that power enables the *ego* to *extend him- or herself* into the *alter*,[25] i.e. to see *him- or herself in the alter*. It provides the *ego* with an uninterrupted *continuity of self*. The pleasure in power, we may assume, derives from this *feeling of continuity*.

Every power space possesses the structure of the self that wants *itself*. Supra-individual structures of power, such as a state, may not rest on the will of an individual, but they also possess the constitution of a self that affirms *itself*. The figure of a head of state reflects the state's structure as a subject. Every power space is a *continuum of a self* that maintains *itself* against another. Continuity and subjectivity are structural elements that are common to all manifestations of power.

Supra-individual power structures also have different forms of mediation, and the relationships between the totality and the individual elements differ accordingly. In the absence of any mediation, the totality overpowers the individual elements. In that case, power must resort to prohibitions or orders. The totality *extends itself* into the elements only by virtue of coercion [*Zwang*]. In the case of intense mediation, by contrast, the formation of continuity takes place without coercion because the individual elements experience the totality as their *own* determination. Nothing is imposed on the individual elements by the totality. Thus, in a law-governed state the individual citizen does not experience the legal order as a form of coercion exerted from the outside. Rather, it represents the citizens' self-determination. It is what *first* turns them into *free* citizens. In a totalitarian state, by contrast, the individual suffers the totality as a determination by an *alien* force. This lack of mediation produces a high degree of coercion. Forced continuity is fragile.

16

If we take the idea of mediation as our point of reference, the various theories of power which are frequently pitted against each other can be subsumed under a common theoretical model. Power as coercion and power as freedom are not fundamentally different; they differ only with regard to the degree of mediation. They are different manifestations of the *one* power. All forms of power aim at the constitution of continuity and presuppose a self. A lack of mediation produces coercion. At the highest point of mediation, power and freedom coincide. That is the situation in which power is as stable as it can possibly be.

Even if a power space achieves a high level of mediation internally, it may still behave antagonistically towards what is external to it, i.e. towards other power spaces. In the case of an extreme lack of mediation, violence may again determine these relationships. Thus, in order to defend its interests, even a democratic state may threaten another state with openly hostile actions or may resort to the use of force. If the antagonistic power spaces are to be united, or *mediated*, into a totality, a sphere of power that includes them both would then be needed.

It is part of the *logic of power* that the formation of supranational power structures – i.e. of a supranational legal order[26] – is necessary for the avoidance of conflicts between nation states. What is needed is a *globalization of power and rights* that overcomes the condition of individual national states. Power must be assigned a *place* that exceeds the separation of individual nation states. The ferocity of globalization derives from the fact that it is not sufficiently global, not *mediated by the world*, that – due to extremely asymmetric structures – it produces unjust distributions of opportunities and resources, and that there is no overall mediating power institution. Out of a dialectical interplay between positive and negative, a mediating structure will emerge and consolidate itself. Thus, globalization needs to go through a *process of dialectical formation*. Hegel would say that globalization is still *without a concept*. Concept means *mediation*. In this context, even the transnational structure of globally active economic corporations may be *one* factor that promotes this mediation process.

The forms of power that we have looked at so far all have a communicative structure. Even the physical violence used to coerce another person into performing a particular action is still part of a communicative process in so far as it realizes a decision regarding a course of action, even if it does so by the use of force. It is used in order to force the other person to do or not to do something. When power, however, is severed from any communicative context, it becomes *naked* violence. The uncanniness and unfathomable nature of violence derives from this nakedness. For instance, the arbitrary torture or the utterly senseless killing of others, carried out without any communicative intention, points towards this *sense*-less, even pornographic, form of violence. Ultimately it does not matter to the perpetrator of a nakedly violent act *what* the other person does. Nor is obedience what matters. Obedience, after all, is still a communicative act. Rather, naked violence attempts *altogether to extinguish* the doing – the will, even the freedom and dignity – of the other. It aims at a complete annihilation of *alterity*.[27]

The archaic practice of power Canetti repeatedly invokes – as if it were the only form of power – also entirely lacks communication:

Mana is the name given in the Pacific to a kind of supernatural and impersonal power, which can pass from one man to another. It is something which is much desired, and an individual can increase his own measure of it. A brave warrior can acquire it to a high degree, but he does not owe it to his skill in fighting or to his bodily strength; it passes

18

into him as the mana of his slain enemy ... The effect of victory on the survivor could not be more clearly conceived. By killing his opponent the survivor becomes stronger and the addition of mana makes him capable of new victories. It is a kind of blessing which he wrests from his enemy, but he only obtains it if the latter is killed. The physical presence of the enemy, first alive and then dead, is essential. There must have been fighting and killing, and the personal act of killing is crucial. The manageable parts of the corpse which the victor removes and either embodies into himself, or wears as trophies, serve as continual reminders of the increase of his power.[28]

This archaic fight need not be preceded by a conflict of interest, which anyhow would give it a communicative character. The only things that matter are the killing of the other and the perception of the killed. The feeling of power emerges without mediation, i.e. without any communicative mediation. And it does not result from the acknowledgement of the strength of the victorious party by the others either. It moves like a magical force from the one killed to the victor.

Archaic consciousness, it seems, reifies power into a substance that one can own. But power is a relation. Thus, without the *alter* there is no power for the *ego* either. The killing of the other ends the power relation. A situation in which two people blindly are attacking each other does not involve power but only differences of physical strength. Power in the true sense only emerges once one of the two opponents submits him- or herself to the other out of the fear of possible death or in anticipation of the other's physical superiority. Power in the true sense is not the fight to the death but the absence of such fighting.

Canetti clearly operates with a very limited concept of power. He mostly identifies it with coercion, repression and subjugation. Thus, the power relation does not go beyond the relation between cat and mouse:

> The cat uses force to catch the mouse, to seize it, hold it in its claws and ultimately kill it. But while it is *playing* with it another factor is present. It lets it go, allows it to run about a little and even turn its back; and, during this time, the mouse is no longer subjected to force. But it is still within the power of the cat and can be caught again. If it gets right away it escapes from the cat's sphere of power; but, up to the point at which it can no longer be reached, it is still within it. The space which the cat dominates, the moments of hope it allows the mouse, while continuing however to watch it closely all the time and never relaxing its interest and intention to destroy it – all this together, space, hope, watchfulness and destructive intent, can be called the actual body of power, or, more simply, power itself.[29]

Power is more 'spacious' than violence. And violence becomes power if it 'gives itself more time'. Looked at from this perspective, power rests on an excess of space and time. In the game of cat and mouse, however, that space is no more than a waiting room before death. The cell of death may be bigger than the cat's mouth, but the space of power that is filled with fear does not provide any room for positive action. In order for something genuinely 'new' to emerge, the 'play' must be more than a playful preparation that leads to the killing. It would need to involve a genuine *room for play* that provides strategic opportunities. Power also presupposes a temporal space that is more than the *not-yet* of the final deadly attack. Obsessed with death, Canetti seems to forget that power does not simply kill, but most of all *lets live*. Because he is fixated on the negativity of power, he does not recognize that power does not rule out actions and freedom, that it *provides time and space* and is not merely a prelude to death. The space-time[30] of *being-able-to* [Können], or of freedom, may ultimately turn out to be an illusion. But power presupposes it, if only in the form of a *semblance*.

2

The Semantics of Power

In contrast to naked violence, power can be associated with *sense*. Through its semantic potential it becomes inscribed in a hermeneutic horizon. But what does *sense* mean? What does it mean to say something has a sense? If A, B and C accidentally stand next to each other, their proximity does not make any sense. Sense only emerges when contingency or pure contiguity, i.e. accidental proximity, is structured by a specific *figure*. A, B and C only participate in something that makes sense if, in some way, they relate to each other, i.e. if they are integrated into a form, a context, a *relational continuum* that relates them to each other. A, B and C become senseless if the form that holds them together completely disintegrates. A world also suffers a total loss of sense if it becomes devoid of all reference. Language is itself a referential structure, and a word or sentence owes its sense to that structure. Similarly, a tool only acquires its sense from a what-for, i.e. from the context of its purpose and function. Thus, sense is a phenomenon of relations and relating. Something only becomes meaningful or makes sense if it is integrated into a net of relations, a continuum or horizon of sense, that lies beyond that thing, and that precedes the apprehension of a thing or event without, however, *itself* becoming an object of conscious perception. The horizon of sense which directs hermeneutic, i.e. topical, intentionality does not need to become topical itself. Power must thus inscribe itself into a hermeneutic horizon, or rather it even needs to form such a horizon itself in order to be able to steer processes of understanding and acting effectively. It only gains stability when it is seen from the perspective of sense or of what *makes sense*. This is what distinguishes it from violence, which is naked because it is stripped of all sense. By contrast, there is no such thing as naked power.

Nietzsche was no doubt the first to provide a striking formulation of the complex connection between power and the production of sense. From a very elementary – even somatic – level on, he connects sense with power. Sense *is* power. '*To communicate oneself*' is 'originally', Nietzsche writes, '*to extend one's power over the other*'.[1] Thus, a sign is 'the (often painful) imprint of a will on another will'. The first form of language is the physical language of injury as an immediate expression of the '*will-to-appropriate*'. The con-*cept* [Be-*griff*] would accordingly also derive from this violent grasp or taking hold. The powerful makes *him-* or *herself* understood through causing injury and through painful 'strikes'. Thus, '*injuries* inflicted on the other' are the '*sign language of the one who is stronger*'. According to this semiotics of power, which, admittedly, is *poor in mediation*, signs are originally wounds. The reception and understanding of this special sign language takes place as a 'sensation of pain and acknowledgment of an alien power' that strives for the '*conquest of the other*'. Quick comprehension aims at 'receiving the fewest blows possible'. Messages are stings; their sense is domination. Understanding means obeying. Nietzsche would probably have claimed that the

23

original intention behind linguistic conjugation [Beugung] was to *bend* [beugen] the will of the other.

Nietzsche conceives of naming as a right of the master. The rulers 'set their seal on everything and every occurrence with a sound and thereby take possession of it, as it were'.[2] The origin of language lies in the 'expression of power by the rulers'. Languages are an 'echo of the *oldest acts of appropriating things*'. Thus, in every word, Nietzsche hears a 'command': From now on, this shall be the name of the thing![3] Naming is at the same time a bestowal of sense. Power founds sense. '"That is how it *should* be!"' is the dictum of the '*true philosophers*' who are '*commanders and legislators*'.[4] Every word is a word of command. The powerful make the originary decision on the sense and the horizon of sense, i.e. the '"where to?" and "what for?"' of all things. They found a *continuum of sense* against the backdrop of which the interpretation of things takes place. For the holder of power, this continuum of sense is at the same time a *continuum of self* in which he or she recognizes *him- or herself*.

According to Nietzsche, sense is not based on a 'how things stand' apart from any inclination; it is not an expression of the world and of things 'as they are' that can be discovered by way of interest-free contemplation. If sense simply rested on how things are, and not on possession or domination, then the name-giver would not be a holder of power but a seer or hearer. Nietzsche's monism of power deprives all things of a simple being-thus. Absence of the will to power would lead to a lack of sense. Thus, sense is not something given that one only needs to receive, nor is it an *event* that *occurs* apart and away from power. Rather, it is a kind of booty. Only power lets things participate in *sense*. In this respect, too, power is anything but mute, *senseless* coercion. It is *eloquent*. It articulates the world by naming things and determining their 'where to' and 'what for'.

Power founds *significance* by forming a horizon of sense against which things are interpreted. Only *with regard to* power do they become *meaningful*, receive a sense. The relationship with power is constitutive of sense. Thus, there is no sense-in-itself: 'Isn't sense necessarily relational sense and perspective? All sense is will to power (all relational sense can be dissolved into that will).'[5] Truth is also associated with power. It is a design or a construction that emerges from the will to power which makes 'a particular kind of untruth victorious and lasting'.[6]

All structures of sense are 'perspectival evaluations ... with the help of which we sustain ourselves in life, that is, in the will to power, to the growth of power'.[7] All purposes and aims are just 'expressions and metamorphoses of the One will', namely the will to power.[8] Processes of sense are processes of power. These processes mean 'that the will to power has achieved mastery over something less powerful and has impressed upon it its own sense of a use function'. Thus, the history of a 'thing' is also a history of power, a 'continuous chain of signs, continually revealing new interpretations'.[9] 'Something-that-wants-to-grow' interprets every other 'something-that-wants-to-grow' with regard to its potential value for the increase of its own power, namely with regard to its *sense*. Thus, the intention *'to become master over something'* lies at the base of 'interpretation'.[10]

Nietzsche's theory of power surely bears polemical traits. But at the same time it is a poetics of power. For his power is 'poetic'.[11] It produces ever-new forms and perspectives. It is not designed for the purpose of a despotic mastery that posits one perspective as the absolute one. The poetics of power possesses a different intentionality. Architects, Nietzsche says, 'have always been under the spell of power'. The most powerful people always inspired architects. Architecture is 'a way for power to achieve eloquence through form'.[12] Power creates forms and manifests itself in forms. It is therefore anything but inhibiting or repressive. By shaping space, the architect creates a *continuum of form* in which he or she is with *him- or herself*. The architect designs *him- or herself* by designing a space. Power lets the architect – the architect's self, so to speak – *become spatial and grow in space*. Power achieves the *extension* of the creating body into the world.

This *extension* may, of course, have violent traits. But it is not, *as such*, violence. Accordingly, power *may* have repressive effects, but it is not *based* on repression. Thus, power is not, as Jakob Burckhardt famously put it, 'of its nature evil'.[13] The demonization of power blinds us, in particular, to its semantic effects, which, according to Nietzsche, transform the naked voice into *language*, i.e. interweave it with sense, in the first place. The problem with Nietzsche's monism of power is rather that he interprets all processes involving sense as also processes of power.

In his analysis of power, Foucault also draws attention to the 'tendency not to recognize the latter [i.e. power] except in the negative and emaciated form of prohibition'.[14] That same general tendency narrows the perspective on Foucault's own theory of power. It is claimed, for instance, that for Foucault the history of power is a 'history of loss',[15] whereas Foucault, in fact, says, with a critical intention, the following:

> Power is essentially that which represses. Power is that which represses nature, instincts, a class, or individuals. And when we find contemporary discourse trotting out the definition that power is that which represses, contemporary discourse is not really saying anything new. Hegel was the first to say this, and then Freud and then Reich. In any case, in today's vocabulary, being an organ of repression is almost power's Homeric epithet.[16]

26

In truth, repression only represents *one* particular form of power, namely the one that is *poor* or *devoid of mediation*. But power itself is not *based* on repression. Foucault repeatedly distances himself from this negative conception of it: 'We must cease once and for all to describe the effects of power in negative terms: it "excludes", it "represses", it "censors", it "abstracts", it "masks", it "conceals". In fact, power produces; it produces reality.'[17] Foucault's power is 'a power bent on generating forces, making them grow, and ordering them, rather than one dedicated to impeding them, making them submit, or destroying them'.[18] On the connection between the body and power, Foucault says:

> What makes power hold good, what makes it accepted, is simply the fact that it doesn't only weigh on us as a force that says no, but that it traverses and produces things, it induces pleasure, forms knowledge, produces discourse. It needs to be considered as a productive network which runs through the whole social body, much more than as a negative instance whose function is repression.[19]

Foucault's references to the productivity of power are rarely acknowledged. He himself is partly responsible for this fact in so far as his analyses of power show a one-sided preference for coercive practices and the paradigm of struggle. In order for the positivity and productivity of power to become visible, he would have needed to analyse it with regard to its semantic potential. Even in *Madness and Civilization* he was still using, as he himself admits, 'a purely negative conception of power'.[20] Apparently, he became aware of the productive effects of power, those effects that even create part of *reality*, only later. From then on, he distrusted the assumption of a 'nature' or an 'essence' that is disfigured or alienated by particular coercive mechanisms or power mechanisms, an essence that would therefore need to be liberated or restored in its purity. The phenomena are all already effects of power. This constitutes Foucault's monism of power: 'The man described for us, whom we are invited to free, is already in himself the effect of a subjection much more profound than himself. A "soul" inhabits him and brings him to existence, which is itself a factor in the mastery that power exercises over the body. The soul is the effect and instrument of a political anatomy.'[21] Foucault liberates power from its narrow conception in terms of prohibition and coercion. But his monism of power limits the dimension of the social. Social *sense* is not exclusively generated by power.[22]

Foucault also questions the repressive hypothesis in the context of sexuality. Sexuality is not a drive that power invariably needs to confront with a *No*. Instead of establishing an aseptic condition, it multiplies the seeds of pleasure. Power does not simply silence sexuality. Rather, it develops a 'discursive erethism'.[23] It renders the body *eloquent*. Probing questions excite new feelings of pleasure. The controlling gaze fixates and intensifies them. Thus, the dispositif of sexuality[24] does not find expression as a prohibiting law but as an 'inciting and multiplying mechanism'.[25] Power does not lead to less but to more pleasure. Relations of surveillance turn into inductive contacts, which electrify the skin. Power shapes a sexual body which incessantly *talks* and *means*. In this way, the semantics of sexual pleasure is tied to the semantics of power in manifold ways. The body is never naked. Rather, it is infused with meanings which, according to Foucault, are effects of power.

The juridical form of power, which sets up prohibitions, does not capture the 'twofold effect'[26] of power: 'Power operated as a mechanism of attraction; it drew out those peculiarities over which it kept watch. Pleasure spread to the power that harried it; power anchored the pleasure it uncovered.'[27] However, Foucault fails to recognize the possibility of power not only rousing pleasure involuntarily but *being effective through pleasure*. In that case, pleasure is not just a side effect of a prohibition. Rather, power specifically produces pleasure in order to be *effective*.

According to Foucault, the juridical pattern of power – i.e. the prohibitions of the legislating power on the one side and the obeying subject on the other – is not capable of describing the 'strategic resourcefulness', the 'positivity' of power.[28] Foucault draws attention to a form of power that cannot be captured in terms of laws, prohibitions, or interdictions, one that is not inhibiting or reducing but creating. It acts 'in the very body and over the whole surface of the social field according to a system of relays, modes of connection, transmission, distribution, etc.'[29] Power appears as a 'multiplicity of force relations immanent in the sphere in which they operate and which constitute their own organization'.[30] Instead of just erecting or destroying barricades, power produces a system of relations, a network for communication that is pervaded by signs and meanings.

In *Discipline and Punish*, Foucault speaks of 'three technologies of power'.[31] These can be characterized with regard to their semantic effects. First, Foucault discusses sovereign power. As the power of the sword, it diffuses from the top to the bottom. Its manifestations are severe; they take the form of revenge or of victory in battle. The criminal is an enemy who needs to be defeated. It has a low degree of differentiation and mediation in so far as its language is limited to a simple *'symbolics of blood'*:[32] 'A society of blood – I was tempted to say, of "sanguinity" – where power spoke through blood: the honor of war, the fear of famine, the triumph of death, the sovereign with his sword, executioners, and tortures; blood was a *reality with a symbolic function*.'[33] Blood *signifies* [*bedeutet*]. The body of the tortured individual also acts as a sign. It is a 'mark', a memorial mark which *signifies*. The power of the sovereign *speaks* through the dismembered body or through the scars left behind on the body by torture. It 'traces around or, rather, on the very body of the condemned man *signs* that must not be effaced'.[34] Torture and torment are carried out as a ritual, as a *staging* that works with signs and symbols.

The second technology of power, the power of civil law, uses a special system of signs: 'it is the mind or rather a play of representations and signs circulating discreetly but necessarily and evidently in the minds of all'.[35] Power produces its effects by letting signs and ideas circulate. It is not the sword but the pen that produces the law. Thus, power does not manifest itself as coercive force but as 'coercive certainty'. It wants to use not terror but reason to bring about its effects. Compared to the sword, the pen places power on more stable grounds. In the following passage, Foucault quotes from Servan, a contemporary of Kant:

> [T]he 'mind' as a surface of inscription for power, with semiology as its tool; the submission of bodies through the control of ideas; the analysis of representations as a principle in a politics of bodies that was much more effective than the ritual anatomy of torture and execution ... Let us hear once more what Servan has to say: 'When you have thus formed the chain of ideas in the heads of your citizens, you will then be able to pride yourselves on guiding them and being their masters. A stupid despot may constrain his slaves with iron chains; but a true politician binds them even more strongly by the chain of their own ideas; it is at the stable point of reason that he secures the end of the chain.'[36]

This form of power is more stable than sovereign power because its effects are not external but internal, i.e. it can do without external coercion: it lets freedom and subjugation coincide.

The power of the pen, or of spirit, is not eruptive. Its quiet effectiveness is owed to respect for moral ideas or the law. Spirit does not count on brute force but on *mediation*. Power, in this case, is not incalculable, irregular, or eruptive, like the power of the sword; it is continual by forming a *continuum* of ideas and conceptions that pervades a society. The power of spirit is the power of the law, and the law is circulated as a 'signifying system'[37] that is perpetually renewed by, for instance, 'a visible punishment, a punishment that tells all, that explains, justifies itself, convinces'.[38] This 'ritual recoding' is done using placards, posters, symbols and texts that are circulated by power at the 'festival of the penal code'.[39] The punishment no longer stages the power of the sovereign. Rather, it is a 'lesson' that serves the purpose of renewing the signifying system. The power that presents itself at the festival of the penal code through so many words and signs, and that inscribes itself into young minds through children's stories, counts on *mediation*, as opposed to the power of sovereignty whose acts are sudden and *unmediated*.

It is not only with the advent of the civil code that the space of power becomes a space filled with sense. The entry of the king in mediaeval times, which represented a ritual affirmation of the union on which power rested, was already a symbolic celebration. It made power appear *meaningful*. Power exerts its effects through the *semblance* of sense. By contrast to this symbolic renewal of the union, the later 'ceremony of torment', with its 'arsenal of terror', is very poor in sense and mediation. But despite being very differently structured with regard to mediation, both forms of power found a *continuum*.

Disciplinary power, the third technology of power, enters deeper into the subject than wounds or ideas. It enters into the inside of the body, so to speak, where it leaves its 'traces' and thereby creates *habitual routines*. It is meant to operate as discreetly and subtly as the power of the penal code, yet more immediately, without taking a detour via ideas. Disciplinary power depends more on reflexes and less on reflection. Foucault derives the birth of the prison from this disciplinary power, which no longer aims at restoring the juridical subject but at shaping 'the obedient subject' by way of the 'training of behaviour by a full time-table, the acquisition of habits, the constraints of the body',[40] by way of a 'concerted orthopaedy'[41] which codes 'as closely as possible time, space, movement'.[42] Because it establishes habitual routines, it can, according to Foucault, 'give up its earlier display'.[43] It now presents itself as *commonplace*.

Disciplinary power speaks a differentiated *language*. It wants to become second nature rather than to hurt. It works with norms or normalities, not with the sword. Foucault also ascribes positivity and productivity to this kind of power. It forms and structures the body, produces new movements, gestures and postures, which are directed at a particular purpose. Out of 'formless clay' it makes a 'machine': 'posture is gradually corrected; a calculated constraint runs slowly through each part of the body, mastering it, making it pliable, ready at all times, turning silently into the automatism of habit'.[44] Given the formative effects of power, a critique of power with the idea of the total liberation of the body from power relations would remain purely *abstract*. Despite the coercion that is associated with disciplinary power, productive effects emanate from it.

Foucault suspects that there is a secret correlation between the body that can be formed and put to use, the body conceived of in the technico-political register, and La Mettrie's *homme machine*, the body conceived of in the anatomico-metaphysical register. The belief in 'docility' is the relay connecting the body that can be analysed with the body that can be manipulated. Disciplinary power not only produces subjugated, obedient, docile bodies, but also entertains relations to the production of discourses. It therefore also creates knowledge. The philosophico-metaphysical discourse of the *homme machine* communicates with disciplinary power. Foucault suggests that we should abandon an intellectual tradition guided by the idea 'that knowledge can exist only where the power relations are suspended and that knowledge can develop only outside its injunctions, its demands and its interests', i.e. we should 'abandon the belief that power makes mad and that, by the same token, the renunciation of power is one of the conditions of knowledge'.[45] Thus, there is no relation of power that does not also constitute a field of knowledge. And there is no knowledge that is entirely free of relations of power.

What is at stake in disciplinary power, Foucault notes, is no longer 'the language of the body', or 'signifying elements', but only the 'economy, the efficiency of movements, their internal organization'.[46] However, disciplinary power cannot be limited to the effects of this economy of force because the body is not only worked on [bearbeitet] by it but also *described* [*beschrieben*] by it.[47] Disciplinary power takes possession of the body by inscribing it into a network of meanings. The 'traces' left by the disciplinary power on the body are always *meaningful*.[48] They inhabit the *soul*.

As opposed to violence, power functions through sense or *meaningfulness*. Even in its violent form, its effect, namely the wound, is a *sign* that *signifies*. The signifying system of the penal code is also a continuum of sense which directs actions with the help of ideas, even if it lacks the heaviness and slowness of sovereign power. Disciplinary power also weaves the 'nexus of habits', which consists of structures of sense.[49]

In a lecture, Foucault says: 'That through which power worked in the 19th century were the habits imposed on definite groups. Power can give up its earlier display. It takes on the wiliest, everyday form of the norm, it conceals itself as power and gives itself out as society.'[50] Power increases its efficiency and stability by concealing itself, by presenting itself as something commonplace, something taken for granted. Therein lies the *cunning of power*. However, this power, which operates without coercion or threats and solely through the 'automatism of habit', is not limited to the nineteenth century. It is operative in every society that shows a sufficient degree of complexity.

The orthopaedic power which Foucault traces in prisons, military barracks or hospitals mostly targets the body. Because it is focused to a large extent on the body, Foucault does not sufficiently take note of the power that creates habits at the symbolic level. Habitus refers to the totality of a social group's dispositions or habits. It comes about through an internalization of values or perceptions that are formed with regard to a particular order of rule. A habitus facilitates a pre-reflective adaptation to this order, an adaptation that is also effective at the somatic level, and it creates automatic habits which mean, for instance, that those who are socially disadvantaged act according to patterns which stabilize the very ruling order that led to them having become disadvantaged. The habitus causes a preconscious affirmation and acknowledgement of the ruling order which is repeated at the somatic level.[51] The things one is forced to do because of one's low social rank are experienced as being done out of *free* choice. The unavoidable is turned 'into a taste of freedom'.[52] An '*amor fati*' forms which 'lets the victims dedicate and sacrifice themselves to the destiny that has been socially allocated to them'.[53] Destiny is experienced as a free project. The one who is dominated even develops a taste for his or her negative condition. Poverty becomes a freely chosen lifestyle. Coercion or repression are experienced as freedom. Habitus directs the action in such a way that the ruling relations of power reproduce themselves, in almost magical fashion, without any rational justification. Bourdieu's theory of habitus also shows that power does not need to appear in the form of coercion. Rather, power is most powerful, most stable, where it creates a feeling of freedom and where it does not need to resort to violence. That freedom may be a fact or an illusion. But in any case, it stabilizes power, is constitutive of power.

Power which establishes or stabilizes itself through habitus works at the symbolic level. Its effectiveness is not achieved 'at the level of physical strength, but at that of sense and knowledge'.[54] It makes use of signs and structures of sense. The aim is to establish a particular view of the world or a particular system of values which legitimizes the rule of a particular group. Those subjected to this power submit to it as if it were a natural order. In this case, power is effective by virtue of the fact that it forms the horizon of sense or understanding of the ruled. It founds a *continuum of sense* in which the ruling social stratum can stay *with itself*. It is therefore at the same time a *continuum of self*. This continuum of power does not operate with prohibitions, but rather through taken-for-granted *understandings* [Selbst-*verständlich*-keiten]. The experience of such sense mostly takes place at a preconscious level. Social sense always contains an element of power and domination. It expresses diverse interests of power. After all, it is a sedimentation of symbolically operating power. Power is never *naked*. Rather, it is *eloquent*. It takes hold by producing perspectives or interpretative patterns which serve the purpose of legitimizing and maintaining a ruling order. Such perspectives or patterns also have effects on the somatic level. As '[p]ractical sense, social necessity turned into nature, converted into motor schemes and body automatisms', social sense makes sure that actions are '*sensible*, that is, informed by a common sense'. Such understanding, however, is immediate, even similar to habitual reflexes. The sense is therefore not questioned: 'It is because agents never know completely what they are doing that what they do has more sense than they know.'[55]

Power not only inscribes itself into a habitus. The nationalization of a mass of people or the formation of a national culture, which take place through symbols or narratives, create a continuum of sense that is used by power. Fragmentation is not helpful to power. The establishment of a homogeneous national structure of sense secures the loyalty of the masses and thus secures power. Hence, the general characteristics of the semantics of power are valid in this context as well.

If we apply the theory of habitus to Heidegger's analysis of 'everydayness' in *Being and Time*, then the latter can be reinterpreted from a sociological perspective.[56] In his phenomenology of everydayness, Heidegger speaks of 'the public way in which things have been interpreted' [öffentliche Ausgelegtheit][57] which determines the 'average understanding',[58] i.e. *normal* perception, the *normal* view of the world. It 'controls every way in which the world and Dasein get interpreted, and it is always right'.[59] Thus, its role is that of a *continuum of sense* or a horizon of sense, which makes sure that things and acts are understood *in a particular way and in no other way*. It provides a particular selection of sense or hermeneutic guidance. The subject of 'average understanding' is simply called the 'they' [Man]. The they [Das Man] sees, acts and judges as *one* [*man*] sees, acts and judges: 'The "they", which is nothing definite, and which all are, though not as the sum, prescribes the kind of Being of everydayness.'[60]

The 'public way in which things have been interpreted' allows for different interpretations. It can be taken to refer to that 'public opinion' which ultimately rests on common convictions or values. From that perspective, it does not necessarily reflect the interests of the powerful rulers. However, the 'public way in which things have been interpreted' can also be understood as that view of the world which provides *orientation*. Dasein is 'disburdened'[61] by it in so far as it does not itself need to interpret or reinvent the world. Being able to find a world that is already *interpreted*, a 'truth' that need not be questioned, amounts to a disburdening of being: 'And because the "they" constantly accommodates the particular Dasein by disburdening it of its Being, the "they" retains and enhances its stubborn dominion.'[62] In both instances, the 'public way in which things have been interpreted' offers a continuum of sense which steers actions and perceptions. Power needs to occupy this semantic space in order to achieve a high level of efficiency and stability.

The 'they', for Heidegger, has an ontological dimension. It simply *'belongs to Dasein's positive constitution'*.[63] The ontology of Dasein does not allow one to ask the question of which power interests, which political processes or economic interests, might be involved in the formation of the 'they', of the 'public way in which things have been interpreted'. Nevertheless, in his description of the 'they' Heidegger uses terms that are charged with the logic of power. Thus, he speaks of the 'dominance' of the 'public way in which things have been interpreted'.[64] It 'keeps watch', Heidegger says, 'over everything exceptional that thrusts itself to the fore'. Every deviation is 'noiselessly suppressed'.[65] This practice of 'levelling down [Einebnung]'[66] has a normalizing effect; it produces an 'average' continuum of sense. Heidegger also mentions 'power':

One belongs to the Others oneself and enhances their power. 'The Others' whom one thus designates in order to cover up the fact of one's belonging to them essentially oneself, are those who proximally and for the most part *'are there'* in everyday Being-with-one-another. The 'who' is not this one, not that one, not oneself [man selbst], not some

37

people [einige], and not the sum of them all. The 'who' is the neuter, *the 'they'* [*das Man*].[67]

The 'dictatorship'[68] of the 'they' does not operate with repression or prohibitions. Rather, it takes the form of the habitual. It is a *dictatorship of what goes without saying*. Power that works through habits is more efficient and more stable than power that gives orders or uses coercion. Its efficiency is based on immanence, on the fact that one *is* the 'they'. One does not suffer the 'they' as coercion. Everyone *is* the 'they'. Bourdieu's 'habitus' possesses a similar structure. Coercion is experienced as freedom, as quasi-natural, because it is *incorporated*.

If we read Heidegger's ontology of everydayness sociologically, we may relate the 'they' to the symbolic power that, according to Bourdieu, produces a 'common sense'. This power brings about its effects by inscribing itself into the public's horizon of sense, thus exerting a normalizing effect, even turning itself into *hermeneutic reflex* which does not require *reflection*. We may think of various constellations of interests, historical processes or relations of production which influence the formation of the 'they'.

The normalization of the 'they' already begins at the affective, even the somatic level. It takes hold of the layer of 'sensitivities', of 'moods': 'Publicness, as the kind of Being which belongs to the "they" … not only has in general its own way of having a mood, but needs moods and "makes" them for itself.'[69] This affective layer of the 'they' gives it a particular effectiveness: it works outside consciousness.

The normalizing power of the 'they' does not rule *over* everyday life. Rather, it operates *out of it*. Its *immanent character* gives it great stability. It works by determining the overall *perspective*, by describing common sense. The place of the sovereign as a particular *someone* is taken by a 'nobody': 'The "*they*", which supplies the answer to the question of the "*who*"

38

of everyday Dasein, is the "*nobody*" to whom every Dasein has already surrendered itself in Being-among-one-other [Untereinandersein].[70] Where it is perceived as *nobody*'s power, i.e. where it is not seen as a *properly* independent entity, power becomes indestructible, so to speak. Where it needs to impose *itself* in the form of repression and exclusion, it is unstable, even 'fragile'.[71]

In everyday being-with-one-another, Dasein 'stands in *subjection* [*Botmäßigkeit*] to Others'. This deprives it of its *independence* [*Selbstständigkeit*]: 'It itself *is* not; its Being has been taken away by the Others. Dasein's everyday possibilities of Being are for the Others to dispose of as they please.'[72] Heidegger opposes this 'dominion of the others',[73] i.e. of the 'they', to 'authentic existence',[74] the 'resoluteness of self' [Entschlossenheit zu sich]. Hence, against the 'dictatorship' of the 'they', the task is to choose *oneself*, to seize *oneself*. The goal is a *sovereignty of the self*. In this context, to be sovereign means to extract oneself from the dictates of the 'they', from the continuum of sense of 'public interpretedness'. Such resoluteness, however, does not lead Dasein beyond what is *factically* given to it, because, Heidegger says, Dasein is *thrown* into 'what is factically possible',[75] into the factically given context of life. Thus, freedom is only possible within the framework of 'thrownness'. Freedom and 'thrownness' do not categorically exclude each other.

Because Heidegger radically separates ontology and sociology, he is unable to appreciate the possibility that 'thrownness' [Geworfenheit] might be a *submission* [*Unterworfenheit*], that the way in which Dasein's 'Being is projected' [Entworfenheit][76] is based on its *submission*. Dasein projects *itself* towards the ruling order by submitting itself to a particular continuum of sense, a particular 'way in which world and Dasein get interpreted'.[77] The proximity of thrownness and submission is not only an 'ontological' but also a sociological one. Heidegger's ontology of everydayness fails to recognize that everyday understandings may be connected to a 'common sense' that is projected by a 'symbolic power'.

Power achieves a high degree of stability when it appears as a 'they', when it inscribes itself into 'everydayness'. What makes power more effective is not coercion but the automatism of habit. An absolute power would be one that never became apparent, never pointed to itself, one that rather blended completely into what goes without saying. *Power shines in its own absence.*

3

The Metaphysics of Power

Asked whether philosophy had anything to say about the human inclination to exert power, Foucault's answer was that the freer human beings are in their relations with each other, the more they enjoy determining the behaviour of others. The more unpredictable the game, the more varied the possibilities of directing the behaviour of others, the greater the enjoyment. In societies in which there is hardly any opportunity for such play, by contrast, the desire for power also diminishes, he said.

Power presupposes a *scope* for actions. Without such scope, there is only violence and coercion. However, the late Foucault's hedonistic, as one might call it, concept of power moves power too much towards the ludic: 'Power is not evil. Power is games of strategy. We all know that power is not evil! For example, let us take sexual or amorous relationships: to wield power over the other in a sort of open-ended strategic game where the situation may be reversed is not evil; it's a part of love, of passion and sexual pleasure.'[1]

Power may be part of playing. And it may itself have play-ful elements. But it is not based on play. Play may even be considered as opposed to power. The desire for more, which, according to Heidegger, is characteristic of power, is any-thing but playful: 'Power itself only *is* inasmuch as, and as long as, it remains a willing to be more power. As soon as such will disappears, power is no longer power, even if it still holds in subjection what it has overmastered.'[2] Life is not self-preservation but self-assertion: 'Life not only exhibits the drive to maintain itself, as Darwin thinks, but also is self-assertion. The will to maintain merely clings to what is already at hand, stubbornly insists on it, loses itself in it, and so becomes blind to its proper essence.'[3] Again and again, Heidegger returns to Nietzsche's saying: 'what man wants, what every smallest part of a living organism wants, is an *increase of power*'.[4]

Going-beyond-itself is the fundamental trait of power. But in so doing, the subject of power does not leave *itself* behind, nor does it lose *itself*. Going-beyond-itself is power's *form of movement*, while at the same time it is a 'going-together-with-itself' [Mit-sich-zusammen-gehen].[5] This unity of beyond-itself and with-itself expands the *space of self*: 'All living beings appear … as a unity of remaining-in-themselves and going-beyond-themselves … The greater the force to go beyond oneself without losing oneself, the greater the power.'[6] The power of living beings consists in continuing themselves beyond themselves, in occupying more space with *themselves*.

Maybe it is indeed the case that Foucault, as he himself frankly admitted, was not very knowledgeable about anthro-pology, about the human soul. Pleasurable play is not the anthropological foundation of power. Nietzsche was probably more familiar with the human soul than Foucault. In one of his fragments, he writes: 'The pleasure of power derives from the displeasure, experienced a hundred times, of dependency, of impotence. If this experience is lacking, then that pleasure is absent as well.'[7] The pleasure in the exercise of power has to do with the traumatic experience of unfreedom and impotence. The feeling of pleasure caused by gaining power is a feeling of freedom. Impotence means being at the mercy of the other, losing one's *self* in the other. Power, on the contrary, means being with *oneself* in the other, i.e. being free. The intensity of the pleasure therefore does not depend on the openness of play or on the diversity of the forms of play. Rather, it can be explained in terms of the continuity of self which grows in parallel with power.

It has often been pointed out that different structures of power exhibit different structures of mediation. Power that is poor in mediation or does not possess any mediating structures at all develops a system of coercion which leads to the repression of the other. In this way, it approximates to violence. On the side of the holder of power, however, it may create a feeling of freedom, because the holder of power affirms *his or her* decision, *his or her* choice, even against the will of the other. The one who is subjected to power does what the holder of power *wants*. Power creates a continuity of self, although in this case it is an *external* continuity because the one subjected to power acts in accordance with the will of the holder of power without *internally* agreeing with the latter. The continuity of his self gives the holder of power a feeling of freedom in so far as his or her will is not interrupted by that of the other. The one who is subservient forsakes, even if only externally, his or her otherness in favour of the holder of power. He or she allows the choice, i.e. the decision of the holder of power, to take place also in him- or herself, against his or her own will which would have made a different choice. The holder of power sees his own will in the other. This perception of one's self in the other is constitutive of the feeling of power. In the one who is subjected to power, on the contrary, this form of power, which is poor in mediation, causes a feeling of unfreedom. It is precisely this asymmetric distribution of freedom that makes this kind of power unstable.

For Nietzsche, power is anything but play: '***Conquering*** – is the natural consequence of an *excess of power … the realization of one's own image in alien material*.'[8] Life is 'imposing your own form'.[9] The *ego* conquers the *alter* by imprinting or imposing its own image on it. In this context, the *alter* behaves like a passive material which merely expresses the will of the *ego*. The exercise of power that consists of 'imposing your own form' enforces a continuity of the *ego* in the *alter*. As a result, the *ego* sees its own image, i.e. *itself*, in the *alter*. Because the *alter* reflects the *ego*, the *ego* returns to *itself* in the *alter*. Due to its power, the *ego* is free, that is, with itself, despite the presence of the *alter*.

Nietzsche is mostly fixated on a form of power that is poor in mediation. 'Imposing your own form' through 'injuring' and 'overpowering'[10] is not the only way to establish the continuity of one's self. Nietzsche's model of power conceives of the *alter* as a *passive* material which suffers the will of the *ego*, or on which the *ego* imposes itself. If, however, the *alter* is taken to be an individual that is capable of autonomous acts and of making decisions, the relationship between the *ego* and the *alter* takes on a far more complex form. In that case, the *alter* can actively integrate the *ego*'s decision or choice into its own designs and realize it as its *own* act instead of merely *suffering* it passively. What the *alter* does thus still corresponds to the *ego*'s will. But this continuity is no longer enforced one-sidedly by the *ego* but *willed* by the *alter*. One might say that the *alter* follows the *ego*'s will voluntarily. The *alter* turns the *ego*'s will into its *own* will. The *alter* thereby also acquires a feeling of freedom. Such a power relation is much more stable than a form of power that is poor in mediation, one in which the party subjected to power behaves like a passive, physical material. Despite the different structures of mediation, the *ego*'s power consists in *both* cases in the fact that it continues itself in the *alter*.

Power is the capacity to be with oneself in the other. It is not an exclusively human property. Hegel elevates it to a feature of the living as such. It distinguishes the living from what is dead:

> The living stands over against an inorganic nature towards which it behaves as its power and which it assimilates to itself. The result of this process is not, as in the case of the chemical process, a neutral product in which the self-sufficiency of both sides standing opposite one another is sublated. Instead, the living demonstrates itself to be something that reaches over and beyond its other [übergreifend über sein Anderes] which is incapable of withstanding its power . . . Hence, in the other, the living is merely connecting with itself.[11]

The power of the living manifests itself in the fact that it does not lose *itself* in the other, that it rather 'reaches over and beyond its other', occupies the other with *itself*, and thereby continues *itself* into its other. The movement towards the other takes the form of a movement to oneself. The organism, Hegel says, is 'a uniting of itself with itself in its outward process', i.e. in its relationship with its other.[12] A living being that does not have the power to unite with *itself* in the other will perish in this, i.e. in the *negative tension* which the other that penetrates the living being produces in it.

For Hegel, power is active at the most elementary level of life. Digestion is already a process of power through which the living makes its other identical with itself. The living establishes an identity with the other, i.e. a continuity of self, by internalizing what is external to it. Digestive inwardness enables the living to turn the external into something internal, i.e. to return to itself in the other.

Interestingly, Hegel describes the activity of spirit by analogy with digestion, thus highlighting an affinity between the two: 'All activities of the spirit are nothing but different ways of leading the external back to the inwardness which is spirit itself; and only through this leading back, this idealization or assimilation of the outward, does the spirit become spirit and is spirit.'[13] The fundamental trait of spirit is internalization. It sublates the other, the outward, into its inwardness, thus remaining *at home with itself* in the other. What it recognizes, or what the understanding seizes, is not external or alien to spirit. It belongs to it. It is *its* content: 'To wit, recognition destroys the external, the alien in consciousness, and therefore is the return of subjectivity into itself.'[14] The internalization or sublation of the outward into the inner connects digestion and grasping [Begreifen]. Eating and drinking, Hegel says, are an 'unconscious seizure [Begreifen]' of things.[15]

In the state of pure intuition, however, spirit is not fully with itself because it is too much *in the external world*. There is no 'return of subjectivity into itself'. The merely intuitive spirit remains engrossed or dispersed in the world: 'At the point of pure *intuition*, we are *outside ourselves* ... Intelligence is *engrossed* in external material, is one with it ... This is why, in intuition, we may become *unfree* to the highest degree.'[16] Spirit is 'unfree to the highest degree' because it is entangled in the external world, lingers with outside things, instead of being with itself.

In the idea, spirit is freer, that is, more *with itself* than in pure intuition. Every idea is *my* idea. In contrast to pure intuition, I am not engrossed in things but explicitly put them *up in front of me*. I rise above the things by severing my direct ties with them, by forming an image of them that is *my* image, remaining within myself throughout the process: 'It follows that spirit posits the intuition as *its* intuition, permeates it, turns it into something *internal* ... and thus free. By way of this introversion [Insichgehen], intelligence rises to the level of the *idea*. The ideational spirit *has* the intuition.'[17] I *have* the intuition. The idea is *my* idea. In *having*, I am not outside, I am *at home with myself*. The idea is something I have; it is *my* possession. Power transforms pure being into a having. It ensures that spirit 'is not dragged into a spatial dispersion, that, rather, its simple self, in all its clarity, runs through this manifold and does not allow it to claim any independent existence itself'.[18] According to this, the power of spirit consists in its ability to engulf the things in its inwardness, to *inflect* [*beugen*] the external and thus make it internal. Through the force of this *inflection* [*Beugung*], spirit *runs through* the manifold world. This *running through that belongs to inwardness* produces a continuum of self.

Spirit which returns into itself in the other inhabits the world as its *inner space*. Being-in-the-world means being-with-oneself. Faced with an object, spirit enlarges its inwardness by embedding the object in it. Spirit returns to itself in the external by *turning* it into something internal. Spirit consolidates *itself*, deepens its inwardness. Hegel also says spirit 'internalizes itself' or 'recollects itself' [erinnert sich][19] by not lingering *outside* in the object, and instead bringing the object into its inwardness: 'By turning the object from something *external* into something *internal*, intelligence internalizes itself. These two processes, the internalization of the object and the recollection [Erinnerung] of spirit, are one and the same thing.'[20] The 'recollection of spirit' means that spirit moves from the object *into itself*. It expands and consolidates its inwardness *around the object* by making it an internal object. This 'internalization' of the object widens spirit's inwardness and therefore strengthens its inwardness: '*Intelligence* turned out to be spirit, a spirit that *moves* from the object *into itself*,

47

recollects itself in the object and recognizes its *inwardness* as what is *objective*.'[21] It is most of all thinking that makes spirit fully free: 'Consequently, the final pinnacle of inwardness is thought. Man is not free, when he is not thinking; for in that case he relates to something other.'[22] The human being is unfree as long as it relates to the other, to the external, i.e. as long as it does not return to itself in the other, as long as the otherness of the other is not sublated into *sameness*. Thinking spirit permeates and illuminates what is other and takes away its otherness. Thus, it produces a *continuum of sameness*. The 'will' also deepens the continuity of self by imprinting its internal on the external, thus trying to ensure the objectivity of its inwardness. Its fundamental trait is the 'return into itself'. From this perspective, the will to power is always the will to one's *self*.

The 'internalization' of the world as the 'recollection of spirit' need not happen by violent means. A violent inclusion, where the external is forced into the internal by an alien power, would only represent an external form of 'internalization', one without mediation. What Hegel has in mind is a *becoming-internal of the external* in which the world is not embedded in an alien inwardness but rather *internalizes itself* into an inner space. Hegel would have said that the power of spirit is anything but violence, that it does not violate or destroy the other, but rather makes appear in the other what the other *in itself* already *is* – that thinking does not make *declarations* but is an *illumination*. The illuminating light radiates no violence. It is a special light which deeply touches *itself* and recognizes *itself* in *what it illuminates*. It has an *eye*.

Power is a phenomenon of inwardness and subjectivity. Someone who only needed to re-*collect* him- or herself, only needed to linger in his or her *interiority* or linger in *him- or herself*, someone who had no outside at all, would be endowed with absolute power. Where *recollection* and *experience* fully

48

coincide, there would be no impotence and no *pain*. Infinite inwardness means infinite freedom and power.

Subjectivity is constitutive of power. An inorganic being may have a centred structure, but it will not develop a structure of power because it is not animated by subjectivity and does not possess inwardness. The space of power is *ipsocentric*. It is inhabited by a self whose intentionality consists of willing-itself. Paul Tillich also connects power with subjectivity and centredness:

> All structures of power are organized around a centre; they have a point toward which they aim, to which all their parts are related ... The more organized a being is, the more its centredness increases, and it reaches its highest point, human self-consciousness, where every individual aspect of experience is related to the centre of the self. This leads to the idea that it is not just that a social group has a centre – that much is obvious, as otherwise it could never act – but that a social group is also an organism, and that the power of a social group can be seen by analogy with the power of biological organisms. The more an organism's different elements are united around an acting centre, the more developed is that organism and the more power of being it has. Therefore, although similar phenomena can also be found in the animal world, man produces the richest, most universal and most powerful social organisms.[23]

For modern biology, as Luhmann observes, the organism is 'no longer a being with a soul whose forces integrate the parts into a whole, but an adaptive system that reacts to changing environmental conditions and events by using its own performance for sensible acts of compensation, substitution, blocking or complementation in order to keep its own structure invariable'.[24] However, the modern idea of the organism does not altogether contradict Hegel's conception of power. The modern organism owes its structural *invariability* precisely to that power which makes it that the organism asserts *itself* under changing environmental conditions and in various instances, i.e. that it behaves unvaryingly. Here, power again creates a *continuity of self* and enables the organism to remain with itself despite the negative tension created by its environment.

All finite beings are surrounded by otherness. Self-affirmation implies that a being must remain with itself when coming into contact with the other. Without this continuity of self it must perish through negativity, that is, the negative tension which the other causes in it. Whoever is incapable of resolving the negativity, of integrating it into him- or herself, does not have the power to *be*. Tillich also derives the power to be from the capacity of the living to overcome negativity or, as he calls it, non-being, i.e. to include it in self-affirmation:

> One has more power to be, the more non-being needs to be overcome, as long as one is able to overcome it. When it can no longer be borne and overcome, then the result is complete powerlessness and the end of all power to be. That is the risk borne by every living thing. The more non-being a living being can bear within itself, the more threatened it is, and the more power to be it has if it is capable of withstanding this threat ... The more non-being a living process can include in its self-affirmation, without being destroyed by it, the more powerful it is.[25]

Power is the capacity of the living not to lose *itself* while being entangled in the other in manifold ways, to continue *itself* throughout negative tensions. Power is 'the possibility of self-affirmation despite inner and outer negation'. By contrast, whoever is incapable of lingering in negativity and including it in him- or herself possesses only minimal power to be. Thus, with regard to the power to be, the neurotic and 'God' are opposites:

> The neurotic is characterized by the fact that he can include only a little non-being within himself. Faced with the danger of non-being, he flees into his small, narrow castle. The average person is capable of bearing a limited amount of non-being in himself, a creative person a large amount, and God, speaking symbolically, an infinite amount. The self-affirmation of a being despite the presence of non-being is the expression of its power to be. With these reflections, we have reached the roots of the concept of power.[26]

Self-affirmation does not need to go along with the repression or negation of the other. It all depends on the structure of mediation. In the case of intense mediation, self-affirmation is not negating or excluding, but integrating. 'God' would represent a figure of the highest point of mediation. A violent criminal, by contrast, would represent a neurotic who can only achieve a continuity of self through the use of violence without any mediation. Thus, neurotic self-affirmation would lead to the negation of the other.

Hegel also believes that neurotic withdrawal into a rigid image of oneself indicates a dearth of power to be. Spirit is 'power only by looking the negative in the face, and tarrying with it'.[27] As Hegel famously puts it, spirit wins 'its truth only when, in utter dismemberment, it finds itself'. The power of spirit creates the continuity of self across the negative tensions which the *other* causes in it. Only in the absence of mediation would spirit repel the other. Thus, a lack of mediation, the absence of the capacity to mediate, leads to a limited, neurotic spirit.

Power that produces a continuity of self through the

internalization of the other *may*, but need not, appear in the form of violence. The relation of mediation between subject and object is decisive in this respect. In Hegel's conception, a high level of intense mediation means that power ceases to be violent at all. As mediation intensifies, the subject no longer destroys its object. Rather – and this is the crux of Hegel's idealism – internalization produces the identity *in-itself* of subject and object. Thus, the object is not altogether the other of the subject. Rather, the object is conceptually close or isomorphically related to the subject. The internalization of the object by the subject *makes* this closeness, which exists *in-itself*, explicit. Grasping [Begreifen], as a form of internalization, does not violate the thing grasped. Rather, as Hegel would say, it reveals something that already exists *in-itself* in the things but which they cannot realize *for-themselves*, i.e. which they cannot elevate to the status of an object of knowledge. From this perspective, the grasping of objects is not a violent appropriation but a *letting-appear* of what exists in them in embryonic form. Internalization is thus not a violation but a reconciliation. It lets something appear that mediates subject and object:

> This comprehension, this encroachment across the other with the innermost self-certainty immediately contains the reconciliation: the unity of thought with the other is present in principle, for reason is the substantial foundation both of consciousness and of the external and natural. Thus the opposing is no longer something other-worldly; it is not of a substantially different nature.[28]

For, Hegel, 'reason' is more than just a subjective order to which the object must be violently submitted. Rather, it is something that is present and effective in the object itself. Thus, in thinking, the subject reveals what is *common* to itself *and* the object, namely the universal. This relation of mediation modifies the structure of power. Power no longer belongs to an individual subject which appropriates an object in order to return into itself in it. Rather, power is the power of the *universal* which manifests *itself* and which *collects individual* beings, i.e. subjects as well as objects, into a totality.

Hegel also defines the 'concept' as a power: 'This is the power of the Concept which does not abandon or lose its universality in the dispersed objective world, but reveals this its unity precisely through and in reality. For it is its own Concept to preserve in its opposite this unity with itself.'[29] The concept is *universal* [*allgemein*] in the sense that it represents what is encompassing and comprehensive, what is common [*gemein*-sam] to *all* the different phenomena of reality. The con-cept [Be-griff] *extends its grasp*, collecting and mediating, through all the manifold phenomena, and forms a totality. It is a con-*cept* [Be-*griff*] in so far as it reaches through everything and thus grasps it in *itself* [durch*greifend alles* in *sich* be-*greift*]. Thus, it is with *itself* in *all* things. Its power consists in this continuity of self. The concept does not lose *itself* in the 'dispersed objective world'. Its effect is like that of gravitation, which collects parts with regard to the *one* centre. The return-into-itself-in-the-other is also a fundamental trait of the concept. For reality is *its* other, in which it manifests *itself* and beholds *itself*.

It has often been pointed out that power takes different forms depending on the structure of mediation. The power of the concept is characterized by intense mediation because the other of the concept, reality, is not repressed by it. Rather, the concept is *inherent* in it. The concept manifests *itself* not *against* reality but *in* it. The power of the concept is devoid of violence. Hegel would say: *violence is without concept*. The more conceptuality power incorporates, the less coercion and violence originates from it. Reality becomes *transparent* through *its* concept. The concept *illuminates* reality, lets reality *begin to be*. The light of the concept does not blind reality because it is reality's *own* light. The illuminating interpenetration of concept and reality is called *truth*. Thus, we may say: *truth is power*.

The power of the concept, of universality, is a '*free* power' in so far as it does not simply subjugate the other, i.e. reality, but releases or frees it into its own essence. Not violence but freedom determines the relation between the concept and its other: 'The universal is therefore *free* power; it is itself while reaching out to its other and embracing it, but without *doing violence* to it; on the contrary, it is at rest in its other as *in its own* ... it relates to *that which is distinct from it* as *to itself*; in it, it has returned to itself.'[30] When the universal reaches out to its other and embraces it, it does not encounter the other's 'no'. Rather, the reaching out and embracing is affirmed by the other as its *own* truth. The other *freely* submits itself and obeys the embracing power. The embracing power is 'at rest in its other as in its own' because there is no resistance coming from the other. It says 'yes' to the embracing power. *Embraced* by the embracing power, it opens up to it. Thus, absolute power does not need to use any violence. It is based on *free* submission.

Foucault holds the thesis that 'man ... is already in himself the effect of a subjection much more profound than himself'.[31] According to this thesis, man owes his identity, his 'soul', to the internalization of a content which, as Hegel would say, *reaches out and embraces* him. He submits to the embracing power by internalizing it and making it the content of his identity. The 'yes' to the embracing other is a *primary* submission in so far as it *constitutes* the identity of the one who submits himself in the first place. Power, in this case, is not repressive or violating. It founds the identity *in the first place*; it founds even the 'soul'. The embracing *may* have violent traits if it is poor in mediation or lacks mediation altogether. However, for Hegel, such a violent embracing would be an embracing *without a concept, without mediation.*

Power does not primarily operate as repression. Hegel perceives it mainly in terms of the dimensions of mediation and creation. Thus, he also describes the creation of the world in terms of the logic of power. God is 'subjectivity', but this subjectivity is not exhausted by the abstract identity of an 'I am I' devoid of any content. God does not rest in 'eternal tranquility and self-containment'.[32] Rather, he expresses *himself* by creating the other, i.e. the world. However, this creation of the other is not a simple transition into the other, but a return into himself. God sees himself in the world as *his* other. He returns into himself in the world. This return-to-oneself-in-the-other is the fundamental trait of power: 'Power is ... a *negative relation to self through the other.*' It is negative because the relation to self takes place through the other, because it is the return-to-self-in-the-other. A purely positive relation to self would be one that carried no relation to the other with it. Thus, Tillich's 'neurotic' would not be capable of a 'negative relation to self'. He or she would lose *him- or herself* in the relationship to the other. The neurotic would lack the power that would make it possible to *reduce [beugen]* the relation to the other into a relation to self. What is decisive for power is this *reduction [Beugung]*, this *turn towards oneself.*

Power promises freedom. The holder of power is free because he or she is capable of being wholly with him- or herself in the other. God, Hegel says, is 'free, because he is the power to be Himself'.[33] God inhabits or builds an *absolute continuum of self.* There is no rupture, no being torn in which he could lose *himself.* He does not know of anything radically other in which he would not be *Himself.* A neurotic may also be described as someone who not only remains in his 'small, narrow castle', but someone coerced to be everywhere with him- or herself, to be everywhere *Him-* or *Herself*. In a certain sense, Hegel's 'God' or 'spirit' would also be a manifestation of that neurosis.

God is power. Hegel's understanding of religion is entirely dominated by the figure of power. For him, it goes without saying that power is the 'fundamental determination' of 'religion as such'.[34] Not for a moment does he consider the possibility that religion may open up a space that withdraws from the logic of power altogether, that religion may be an experience of *continuity* that differs fundamentally from the *continuity of self* that is produced by power, that religion might represent the very movement that is anything but a return-to-self.

Religion is awakened by the experience of finitude. It is crucial that human beings, as opposed to animals, are explicitly *conscious* of their finitude, that they are able to make their finitude an object of *knowledge*. Thus, the *pain* leads beyond the immediate sensation to a *universal* idea of finitude. The fact that human beings are able to *mourn* and *cry*, that – as opposed to animals – they have religion, also derives from this ideational faculty. Part of the experience of finitude is an experience of individuation, which leads to a fundamental loneliness. In light of the consciousness of one's finitude, a desire arises to overcome the painful experience of the *limitation* of one's existence and to break out of the loneliness of individuation. Religion is based on the experience of one's *limitedness* and *individuation* and the desire to overcome them.

The experience of finitude and of limitedness is not necessarily situated at the level of power. The limitedness of human existence need not be that of power. The experience of limited power is only one possible form of the experience of human finitude. Suffering from finitude may just as well take the form of suffering from the *limit* that separates me from the other and that can only be overcome by the creation of a specific continuity. The continuity that overcomes the separating limit has another structure than the continuity of *self* that is produced by power. It does not possess the *intentionality of a return-to-self*. The limit-less space, the limitless continuity of *being*, is not animated by the self whose striving only aims to be united with itself in the other. It is not power, not the return-to-oneself, that promises salvation, but the departure towards a limitless openness. From this perspective, religion would rest on a desire for the removal of limitations, for an infinity which would, however, not be infinite power. Religious *being unto infinity*, unto the limitless, may no doubt be charged with a *desire* for limitless power, with a boundless *will* to power. But it is not *based* on such a desire. Religion at its roots is *deeply peaceful*. It is *friendliness*.

It is problematic that Hegel describes all religious phenomena purely in terms of an economy of power. A power calculus determines all religious communication. In the case of sacrifice, for instance, one first of all acknowledges 'that one is in the *power of the other*'. At the same time, one exerts power over the other by demanding an effect. The invocation of one's acknowledgement of the power of the other and of the consciousness of one's own power dominates the practice of sacrifice. Would it not be possible to conceive of sacrifice as having a much deeper meaning that lies outside the horizon of purposive rationality and utility?

Georges Bataille has a radically different understanding of sacrifice. He does not deny the economic dimension of sacrifice. But according to him the deeper meaning of the sacrifice lies outside economic calculation. Sacrifice represents an antithesis to utility and economy. It is, *at bottom*, a particular kind of destruction and consumption: 'To sacrifice is to give as one gives coal to the furnace.'[35] The act of sacrifice returns the sacrificed object to the state of continuity in which there is no limitation, no separation between subject and object, between human being and world. It is an act of *de-reification* and of the *removing of limits*. The thing is removed from the context of usefulness and purpose. It is thus given back its secret. Bataille's name for the *limit*-less continuity as the proper dimension of religion is 'intimacy' or 'immanence'. Thus, his sacrificer declares: 'I withdraw you, victim, from the world in which you were and could only be reduced to the condition of a thing, having a meaning that was foreign to your intimate nature. I call you back to the *intimacy* of the divine world, of the profound immanence of all that is.'[36]

The continuum of power is a continuum of *self*. As opposed to power, religion is tied to the experience of a *limit*-less continuum of *being*. It is a 'return to the moment' when the human being 'was one with the universe, and differed neither from the stars nor the sun'.[37] According to Bataille, the shudder one feels when confronted with the divine is caused by the violence in the removal of limits, a violence which overcomes differences: 'The sacred is exactly comparable to the flame that destroys the wood by consuming it. Like an unlimited fire, it is the opposite of a thing; it spreads, it radiates heat and light, it enflames and blinds, and the one enflamed and blinded by it suddenly also is a blinder.'[38]

The experience of the undivided unity of being, which Bataille frequently invokes, is orgiastic and regressive. Tellingly, his conception of a philosophy of religion sets out from 'animality'. Animals, he says, already live in a continuity of being. They are in the world 'like water in water'.[39] Therefore, they have no need for religion. They already rejoice in the continuum of being.[40] In the undivided unity of being no power relations can form because power relations presuppose a difference: 'There is nothing in animal life that introduces the relation of the master to the one he commands.'[41] Not even the consumption of the other is preceded by a battle or an 'appropriating-of-the-other'. In the continuum of being there is simply no separation between self and other. There is no assimilation or appropriation in the strict sense of these terms, for these would follow the formula of the logic of power, i.e. they would be a return-to-self-in-the-other. The undivided unity of being does not allow for the separation between the eater and the eaten: 'What is given when one animal eats another is always the *fellow creature* of the one that eats. It is in this sense that I speak of immanence.'[42]

While Bataille's continuity of being excludes power relations, it is perfectly amenable to orgiastic forms of *violence* which remove limits and destroy, and which evade any sense or purposive context. The 'divine', which Bataille compares to the all-consuming flame, is also completely present in these orgiastic excesses of violence. Thus, the divine is anything but friendly. 'Intimacy' also takes away the *openness* from the continuity of being.

As Bataille recognized, religion rests on an experience of continuity. But this experience is a phenomenon of *spirit* which goes far beyond Bataille's imaginary 'animality'. *Spirit* is *friendliness* in so far as it founds a *continuity of being* without, however, letting differences or *forms* dissolve in an all-consuming flame. This friendliness means that spirit is anything but orgiastic or consuming.

In his *Essay on Tiredness*, Peter Handke refers to a *deep* tiredness in which the self retreats in favour of the world. The depth of this tiredness is that of the world that is received as 'the more that lies in a less of the self'.[43] Dasein is no longer dominated by the *pathos of the self*. In deep tiredness, which excludes the possibility of any care for the *self*, a continuity of *being* opens up.[44] 'The other', Handke says, 'becomes I'.[45] The compulsion to join with oneself in the other, to stay with oneself in the other, gives way to a serene composure.[46] It is

59

part of deep tiredness that 'no one and nothing "dominates" or "commands"'.[47]

Deep tiredness *inspires*: 'The inspiration of tiredness tells them not so much what should, as what need not, be done.'[48] Hegel's 'God', who means 'subjectivity, activity, infinite actuality', 'infinite power', would never fall into deep tiredness. Hegel's spirit, we should not forget, is nothing but a *'doing'*, an *'absolute intervening'*.[49] This spirit can never be tired. Deep tiredness is probably a counter-figure to the power and subjectivity which constitute Hegel's 'spirit'. Handke invokes an altogether different *spirit*, a *religion of deep tiredness*. The 'Pentecostal company that received the Holy Ghost', he writes, was in a state of deep tiredness.[50] Here, spirit reconciles and unites. Nothing stands in complete isolation; everything is 'always in conjunction with other things'.[51] The *spirit* that awakens in deep tiredness is nothing other than *friendliness*: 'Alright. It is also my last image of mankind, reconciled in its very last moments, in cosmic tiredness.'[52]

4

The Politics of Power

'Sovereign', writes Carl Schmitt in his *Political Theology*, 'is he who decides on the exception'.[1] In the state of exception, legal norms are suspended for the purpose of self-preservation. In the case of an exception, an order *prior* to the law, a pre-legal *space* of power which *provides order*, becomes manifest. Thus, the state continues to exist while the law withdraws.

The *theological* sovereign who *decides* in the state of exception possesses an *absolute* power which rules prior to any positive legal norm. No one can raise any matters with him [ihn belangen]. In the state of exception, he decides what matters [was von Belang ist] in the interests of self-preservation. And self-preservation, in that case, becomes what *matters absolutely* [*absoluter Belang*]. The sovereign rises above the legal norm and decides on its validity. He is the subject taking the ultimate decision: 'The decision frees itself from all normative ties and becomes in the true sense absolute.'[2] This sovereignty is nothing but the subjectivity which wills *itself*, which is determined to realize *itself*. The state of exception manifests this *determination* to realize itself in the purest form. This determination is part of any space of power. And only the one who has the power can turn the emergency of threatening self-alienation around and remain with *him- or herself*. The state of exception is the decisive attempt at a return-to-oneself.

In his *Political Theology*, Schmitt quotes from Kierkegaard, who puts the exception above the general. The exception, according to Kierkegaard, thinks the general 'with intense passion'.[3] It 'reveals everything more clearly than does the general'.[4] Accordingly, it is not the normal case but the exception that reveals the nature of sovereignty. However, reflection on the normal case can bring more to light than Schmitt or Kierkegaard believe.

Hegel, the ingenious philosopher of the normal case, who thinks the general with an intense passion, illuminates the nature of sovereignty by looking at the normal case. He claims that 'all that is required in a monarch is someone to say "yes"'.[5] With this he means the 'highest instance of formal decision', i.e. the *formal* sovereign whose 'yes' provides the law with its validity. This 'yes' is the exact equivalent of the 'no' with which the sovereign suspends the law in the state of exception. The 'no' is also an expression of unconditional self-affirmation. Thus, in both cases what we see is an expression of a '*subjectivity* which is certain of itself',[6] i.e. that of the sovereign or the state, an absolute '*self-determination* [of the will] in which the ultimate decision is vested'.[7] The activity of this sovereign consists in the repetition of his *name* and of 'I will'. What matters is this *name*: 'it is the ultimate instance and *non plus ultra*', that is, the 'the self-determining and completely sovereign will, the ultimate source of decisions'.[8] 'I will', even 'I will myself', this determination to self [Entschlossenheit zu sich] embodies the subjectivity of the sovereign, of the one who is '*entirely self-originating*'[9] and who accounts for the existence of the state. Thus, the will of the sovereign speaks not only in the state of exception but also in the normal case. The 'no' in the case of a state of exception may be more *striking* than the 'yes' that is continuously pronounced. But both the 'yes' and the 'no' are expressions of the *will to self*, of the subjectivity that is constitutive of the state as a space of power.

The formal but at the same time theological sovereign must be distinguished from the actual *political* sovereign, who, as a human being, is in constant fear of losing his or her power. As opposed to the theological sovereign, the political sovereign possesses only relative power. Schmitt draws attention to this kind of monarch, a monarch who slides into a fatal dialectic of power:

> The human individual, in whose hand the great political decisions lie for an instant, can only form his will under given presuppositions and with given means. Even the most absolute prince is reliant on reports and information and dependent on his counsellors ... Thus every direct power is promptly subordinated to indirect influences.[10]

Around the holder of power an 'antechamber' forms, which is populated by ministers, father confessors, personal physicians, secretaries, chamber servants and mistresses, and which threatens to undermine the actual power chamber and to fill it with intrigue and lies. The antechamber of power completely cuts the holder of power off from the world, so that 'he is only able to reach those who rule him indirectly, while he can no longer reach all remaining humans over whom he exercises power, and they, in turn, can no longer reach him'.[11] Again, Schmitt bases his reflections on states of exception. The exception may allow us to think the general with intense passion. But this passion may also disfigure or conceal the general. The thesis of the 'isolation of the holder of power through the unmitigated apparatus of power' does not take into account the constitutive effect of that apparatus, i.e. the *structural, constitutive distribution, the spatialization* of power. The apparatus of power does not necessarily take the form of an antechamber of power that undermines the power chamber. After all, an *organized* apparatus of power is necessary for the exercise of political power. In the *normal case*, it is anything but the 'fog of indirect influence'. In addition, in parliamentary democracies we do not find this concentration of power at the top or embodied in one person, and there is no 'corridor to the soul of the holder of power' to which only few people are granted access.[12] The old antechamber of power gives way to other antechambers of power, such as that foyer or vestibule of power called the *lobby*.

For Schmitt, the dialectic of power, which turns power to impotence, suggests that power is 'an objective, autonomous factor' which humans cannot appropriate.[13] The complexity and anonymity of organizations in modern societies tempts Schmitt into suggesting the thesis that the 'reality of power greatly exceeds the reality of the humans'.[14] The neat formula *homo homini homo* is therefore no longer valid. Power also 'transcends all inter-personal measures of every thinkable power of humans over humans'.[15] The relocation of power in a super-human reality is Schmitt's reaction to the fact that 'power and impotence are no longer set over against one another eye-to-eye and no longer gaze at each other from human to human',[16] to the fact that the power of the individual holder of power degenerates into 'the perspiration of a situation' within a 'system of incalculably enhanced division of labor'.[17]

Schmitt apparently lacks the ability to account in theoretical terms for a situation in which power evades the grasp of *one* human individual. Instead of assuming that modern societies subject power to a radical process of distribution or decentralization, he hypostasizes power into an 'independent reality' to which the human being is subjected and which draws the human being into a fatal dialectic. The human being is no longer sovereign because power evades the human will, because the human being can no longer *decide*. The only thing left to Schmitt is *to invoke the human being*: '*To be human, nonetheless, remains a decision.*'[18]

Schmitt's separation of chamber and antechamber, of direct power and indirect influence, is not without its problems. The antechamber of power, which participates in power, is, after all, a part of the power chamber. The fog of indirect influences is only able to undermine the power chamber and occupy the vacated space because it becomes a power chamber itself. That 'hospital room, in which several friends sit about the bed of a paralyzed man and rule the world' is a powerful power chamber.[19] The antechamber is really a side room. The formation of the *side rooms* of power bears witness to the fact that no space of human power can completely seal itself off and remain absolutely *with itself*. Due to its finitude, human power is constantly exposed to the danger of self-alienation. Because of the lack of *closedness*, no human power space is free of side rooms, ante-rooms or surrounding rooms. They are its *wounds*, so to speak. From this finitude of human power the dialectic of self-affirmation and self-alienation follows.

Schmitt's theory of the antechamber of power contains an interesting reference to the dependence of power on *information*. On Bismarck's request to be released from his office as chancellor in March 1890, he writes:

The old, experienced Reich's chancellor, the creator of the Empire, confronts the inexperienced heir, the young King and Kaiser Wilhelm II. Between both of them there existed many material oppositions and differences of opinion in questions of internal and external politics. But the kernel of the petition for release [Entlassungsgesuch], the real point of contention, is something purely formal: the conflict concerning the question of how the Chancellor may inform himself and how the King and Kaiser should inform himself. [20]

The media, which have taken on entirely different dimensions since the time of Bismarck, have also changed the conditions to which *political information* is subject. The media find it easy to cross informational barriers. The formation of an antechamber to power that could cut the power chamber off from the public altogether is inconceivable under these circumstances. Modern information technologies would very quickly perforate such an antechamber of power.

Despite their strong presence in politics, the media *as such* have no power in the proper sense. Talk of 'the power of the media' is therefore misleading. Rather, the media – to use a Schmittian formulation – form a fog of indirect influences. They lack an unambiguous intentional structure. The space of the media is too diffuse and dispersed. When viewed together, they are not led by a particular actor or institution. The structural dispersion and distraction [Streuung und Zerstreuung] immanent to the media do not allow for unambiguous ascriptions. There are too many actors and too many different institutions populating the space of the media. The internet space has no *orientation* at all, which leads to a radical increase of contingency. Moreover, it is useful to distinguish between power and influence. A power that is not able to exert any influence is certainly no power at all. But influence does not always take the form of power. It is not necessarily tied to the formation of a continuum. Influence can be exerted at particular *points*, while power is a phenomenon of *space*. The media do not automatically organize themselves into *one* space of power. But various interactions between the media and power processes are possible. The media can be put into the service of power strategies and their actions. But they can also have a destabilizing influence on ruling power regimes. This is the reason why totalitarian powers try to occupy the space of the media. And the formation of public opinion cannot be considered separately from the development of the media.[21]

In his unwavering orientation towards the exception and towards the proliferating antechambers of power, Schmitt forgets to ask to what extent power is a phenomenon of space. The formation of antechambers of power tells us very little about the functioning of the power-*space* itself.[22] In some respects, there may be a concentration of power at the top or in one person, but it cannot be *based* on this top. In order to be power, it needs a *space* that carries it, affirms it and provides it with legitimacy. *Even if* concentrated at the top, power is an event taking place in a space, in a togetherness or totality. Separation and isolation are detrimental to power. With violence, by contrast, they go well together, because violence takes place *at a particular point*. It may contribute to the creation of power, but power is not based on it. Violence cannot *spatialize itself*.

Power creates a continuum. This applies to a relationship between two people as much as to the polis. If the *ego* were a completely isolated individual, he or she could only break the will of the *alter* through the use of violence. In such conditions of isolation, the *ego* has no power over the *alter*. It is precisely because of the lack of power that the *ego* violates the *alter*. Violence is therefore a sign of *impotence*. If, by contrast, the *alter* would submit to the *ego* of his or her own volition, the ego would possess a lot of power. In that case, the *ego* would continue him- or herself in the *alter* without resorting to violence. By virtue of power, the *ego* is with him- or herself in the *alter*. Power forms this *continuity*; it *spatializes* the *ego*, or rather the *ego*'s will. Violence and violation, by contrast, deepen *rifts* and reduce *spaces*. Power also founds continuity in constellations without one central actor. It forms the gravitational field of a totality that connects and mediates parts with each other.

In the case of a revolution, for instance, violence may certainly play a role. But it fizzles out as long as it is *merely* violence and not associated with any *power*. Without power and without affirmation from *others*, violence is doomed to fail. If, by contrast, it has power, it founds a *new space*. Violence may *capture space*, but it does not *create* space. It may also play a constitutive role in the *emergence* of a political space, but the political is not therefore *based* on violence. Rather, it is based on a *common* will which creates a *continuum* of actions. In this sense, Hegel writes: 'although the state may *emerge* through *violence*, it nevertheless is not based on it ... In the state, the spirit of a people, morality and the law are what rules.'[23] For Hegel, the power of *spirit* consists in the generation of a *we*, a commonality [Gemeinsamkeit], a continuity of what is general and *common* [des All-*gemeinen*]. *Spirit is power* in so far as it founds an emphatic being *together* which rests on a determination to *self*. Violence lacks precisely this power of mediation, i.e. it lacks *spirit*. Only power can create the political.

Hannah Arendt is presumably aware of the spatial aspect of power when she writes: 'What can never grow out of [the barrel of a gun] is power.'[24] From the narrowness of a gun's barrel no space can emerge. It is fundamentally a very lonely place. What creates space and power, by contrast, is legitimation by others. The term 'non-violent power' is, accordingly, not an oxymoron but a pleonasm.[25] An isolated individual may well possess force or strength, but it can never create power all *by itself*. Arendt derives power from being together as such:

Power springs up whenever people get together and act in concert, but it derives its legitimacy from the initial get together rather than from any action that then may follow. Legitimacy, when challenged, bases itself on an appeal to the past, while justification relates to an end that lies in the future.[26]

For Arendt, too, power is a phenomenon involving a continuum. The political presupposes a continuum of acting.

Arendt's concept of a 'space of appearance' makes the spatial character of power topical. According to Arendt, the *polis* is a 'space between',[27] a 'space of appearance', which 'comes into being wherever men are together in the manner of speech and action'.[28] This is a space of being together 'where I appear to others as others appear to me, where men exist not merely like other living or inanimate things but make their appearance explicitly'.[29] The space of appearance is a space which clears itself [sich lichtet] in the course of speaking and acting together. Arendt brings power and the space of appearance into immediate contact: 'Power is what keeps the public realm, the potential space of appearance between acting and speaking men, in existence.'[30] Power is the light which illuminates the *political space* in which acting and speaking together takes place. Arendt uses the concept of 'power' very emphatically and in a positive sense. Thus, she speaks of the 'splendour attending [power's] space of appearance, because power serves appearance and semblance',[31] or of 'the brightness of the public created by power'.[32] Appearing is more than existing. It means *being operative [Wirken]* in an emphatic sense. Thus, power alone creates a 'sense of reality' in addition to a 'sense of life'.[33]

This concept of power, which surely deserves to be called 'communicative', is of course agreeable to Jürgen Habermas. Quoting Arendt, he makes the communicative production of a common will the fundamental phenomenon of power:

Hannah Arendt proceeds from a different model of action, the communicative: 'Power corresponds to the human ability not just to act but to act in concert.' The basic phenomenon is not the instrumentalizing of another's will for one's own purposes but the formation of a common will in a communication aimed at agreement.[34]

Power emerges from the between: 'no one really possesses power; it "springs up between men when they act together and vanishes the moment they disperse"'.[35]

Arendt's theory of power sets out from a very formal level. Power sets free the space of appearance as such, even the sense of reality as such. Where human beings act together, there *is* power. The political is founded on the basis of this common action, which creates power. This rather formal or abstract concept of power certainly has its own appeal. But the question is whether power can really be derived from common action as such or if *something else also has to be present* if the space of appearance is to become a *space of power*.

Were we to follow the communicative model of power to its logical conclusion, then the highest form of power would be a perfect unity in which *everyone* acts in unison. But that is not Arendt's definition of the highest form of power: 'The extreme form of power is All against One, the extreme form of violence is One against All.'[36] This definition seems plausible for the extreme form of violence: 'One against All'. Violence is a *lonely* act. It is not supported by the affirmation by others. The opposite pole, the extreme form of power, would then be: everyone agrees in unison. But Arendt's definition of it is: 'All against One'. Whence this 'against'? In what sense does the extreme form of power that would result from the agreement of all still need an 'against' or a 'One' against whom all others act? What does this lack of clarity in the definition reveal? To which central characteristic of power does this 'against', which has slipped into the definition of power, point? This 'against' is probably an indirect reference to the fact that power is not primarily a phenomenon of togetherness but of the self, that every power structure possesses a subjectivity, a determination to *self* which, however, only manifests itself in the presence of an *Against* within or without the power structure. The self is here taken in an abstract sense. It not only refers to the self of a human individual but to the subject of willing-*oneself*, or of the return-to-*oneself*, which may also pertain to a group.

The very moment that a collective decides to act in unison, a common self is formed which wills *itself*, which is determined to maintain *itself*. This subjectivity, this determination to maintain *itself*, becomes visible in particular when 'someone' opposes the collective. The power of the collective is not *based* on this *one* Against. But where an Against comes into negative contact with the totality, this totality manifests its determination to maintain itself, i.e. it shows the self that is proper to any power structure, be it an individual holder of power or a collective. Where there is a determined Against, a *contraction of power into itself* takes place, as in a state of exception. The power seeks to maintain *itself*. The determination to maintain itself is based on a will to self. Without such a will to self, no power structure comes into being. A minimal subjectivity which *repeats itself* must be assumed to form the basis of any form of power. Only this subjectivity can transform a space of being into a space of power.

Arendt's theory of power sets out from acting together as such. But it does not remain at this synergetic-communicative level. Rather, it proceeds to a strategic-polemical level, without this transition being made plausible in theoretical terms. Thus, in the definition of the extreme form of power, an *Against* appears that cannot be derived from acting together as such. All of Arendt's examples of power have a strategic-polemical character. They point towards another constitutive element of the political, for the political cannot be reduced to acting together.

In his reading of Arendt, Habermas ignores the internal inconsistencies of Arendt's concept of power and reduces it to its communicative aspect. He believes that it is possible to derive the idea of communicative power from a reading of the following passage from Arendt: 'No one really possesses power; it springs up between men when they act together and vanishes the moment they disperse.'[37] But Habermas does not take into account the passage which immediately follows these words of Arendt's. It reads:

> A comparatively small but well-organized group of men can rule almost indefinitely over large and populous empires and it is not infrequent in history that small and poor countries get the better of great and rich nations … the power of the few can be greater than the power of the many.[38]

The lesson to be drawn from this is that acting together is strategic action, i.e. a success-orientated form of acting. This makes organization and strategy necessary. Only through an effective organization and a good strategy may a group that is comparatively small be more powerful than one that is larger.

That power cannot be based on communication and understanding alone also becomes clear when looking at the other examples Arendt mentions in the course of differentiating between power and violence: 'Even the most despotic domination we know of, the rule of master over slaves, who always outnumbered him, did not rest upon superior means of coercion as such but upon a superior organization of power – that is, upon the organized solidarity of the masters.'[39] There can be no talk of communicative power in this case. The 'opinion' of the slaves by itself does not have any power in the face of the organization and strategy of the masters. The slaves are unable to organize themselves or to develop a strategy. The power of the masters over the slaves is the power of a group that owes its existence to a 'superior organization', i.e. an effective strategy. It is not a *communicative* form of power that aims at reaching understanding but a *collective* power orientated towards achieving success.[40] Habermas nevertheless reduces collective power to an effect of communication orientated towards reaching understanding: 'Arendt dissociates the concept of power from the teleological model of action: power is formed within communicative action; it is a group effect of speech in which agreement is an end in itself for all parties.'[41] If understanding were indeed the only end, an end in itself, then no space of power would form.

Again and again, Arendt – probably in part despite her actual intentions – links power with organization and strategy:

> Hence, in domestic affairs, violence functions indeed as the last resort of power against criminals or rebels – that is, against individuals who, as it were, refuse to be overpowered by the consensus of the majority. [It is normally the superior power of this majority and its 'opinion' that orders, or legally enables, the police to proceed with violence against those who ignore its dictum.] And even in actual warfare, we have seen in Vietnam how an enormous superiority in the means of violence can become helpless if confronted with an ill-equipped but well-organized opponent who is much more powerful.[42]

As so often in Arendt, the argument in this passage is not clear. First, she speaks of the power of the state, which is based on 'the consensus of the majority'. Then she moves abruptly from talking about the constitutional state to talking about war, i.e. from the power of the state to the instrumental use of power in times of war, a power which she would like to be taken as distinct from the power of 'opinion'. But at this point she again highlights the positive interaction between power and *organization*. This power of organization cannot simply be reduced to the power of 'opinion'. It has a strategic quality.

Because of his exclusive concentration on communicative power, Habermas does not appreciate this closeness between power and strategy either:

> [F]or Arendt, too, it [strategic action] is essentially apolitical ... The craft of making war is obviously a matter of the calculated employment of means of violence, whether to threaten or to physically conquer the enemy. The accumulation of the means of annihilation, however, does not make the superpowers mightier – military might (as the Vietnam War has shown) is often the counterpart of internal weakness. In addition, the example of strategy is ideal for subsuming strategic action under instrumental action ... And, since the purposive deployment of military means seems to have the same structure as the use of instruments for producing objects or transforming the goods of nature, Arendt, in a kind of shorthand, equates strategic action with instrumental action. She demonstrates that in the waging of war strategic action is as violent as it is instrumental; an action of this type stands outside the realm of the political.[43]

In the context of her example, Arendt also thinks of war in *political* terms. Part of the political is the strategic, which, however, is not identical with the instrumental. Habermas, by contrast, claims that Arendt, 'in a kind of shorthand, equates strategic action with instrumental action'. But this is precisely not the case in Arendt's examples. They show, on the contrary, that strategic action *cannot* be subsumed under instrumental action. How might Habermas seek to explain the victory of the Vietnamese? In what does their power consist? Arendt explains their success with reference to superior organization. They are 'ill-equipped but well organized'. Thus, their success *also* has a strategic character. After all, we are talking about a *war*. Habermas, though, wants to decouple the strategic and the instrumental from communicative power. But communicative power by itself never produces victory. The example of the Vietnam War is a perfect illustration of a victory on the basis of strategy. Habermas's strict separation of communicative power and instrumental violence is problematic. It renders invisible those *strategic intermediate spaces* in which the political resides.

According to Habermas, the fundamental phenomenon of power is 'the formation of a common will in a communication aimed at agreement'. However, this consensus-based model reduces the processes of power substantially. Habermas turns *one* aspect of power into the 'fundamental phenomenon of power'. Yet the asymmetrical relationship between the subject that commands and the one that obeys is *also* a relationship of power. And it does not rest on communication aimed at agreement. On the contrary, power within the relationship between two individuals works against such communication. It rather *declares*. The urge to act in unison with the other is, in turn, not necessarily based on an urge to power.

Habermas's communicative model of power ignores the strategic and polemical dimensions of power. A theory of power which, by contrast, is only informed by the aspect of struggle[44] misses the communicative or collective dimension of power, which is based on collective action, on the formation of a common will and a common self. It is not particularly helpful to take consensus one moment and struggle the next as the 'fundamental phenomenon of power'. It would make more sense to present the consensus-based model and the

75

struggle-based model as two *different variations of one and the same power*. What is therefore needed is an explanatory model which takes account of 'the instrumentalizing of another's will for one's own purposes' *as well as* of 'the formation of a common will in a communication aimed at agreement' as different forms in which power manifests itself.

Subjectivity and *continuity*, or *self* and *continuum*, are two structural moments which are invariable components of all models of power. Power is the *ego*'s capacity to *continue* itself in the *alter*. This capacity founds a *continuum of self* in which the *ego* can remain uninterruptedly with him- or herself. A political power structure, such as a state, is also a *continuum* that generates an overarching order. It also exhibits the structure of subjectivity; after all, the collective presents itself as a *self*. It preserves or affirms *itself*. Figures such as a head of state or a sovereign make these structures of subjectivity visible.

The model of struggle as well as the model of the collective, or of consensus, is based on the structural aspects of power mentioned above. Common decisions, or 'agreement of many wills and intentions',[45] produce a *continuum of actions* based on a *collective self*. Power relations based on struggles also exhibit the two structural moments of power. The victorious party continues *itself* in the defeated party. Thus, it remains with *itself* in the defeated other. Power thus provides it with a *continuum of self*. *With regard* to these structural moments of power, the struggle-based and consensus-based models of power are no longer opposed to each other. However, neither model appears in its pure form. Struggles, for instance, if they take place between groups, presuppose that the members of each group act in concert. By the same token, there is no acting together that is entirely free of polemical or strategic actions. Any plurality of wills modulates communication by introducing strategic considerations.

Having clearly separated strategic action from power as a 'group effect' of communicative action oriented towards reaching understanding, Habermas attempts to reintroduce the latter as part of political action. The expansion of the political to include the strategic is meant to give a 'realistic twist'[46] to the communicative production of power:

> The concept of the political has to be extended to include the strategic competition for political power and the use of power within the political system. Politics cannot, as with Arendt, be identical with the praxis of those who discourse together in order to act communally. Conversely, the dominant theory narrows this concept to the phenomena connected with the competition for and the allocation of power and does not do justice to the peculiar phenomenon of the engendering power.[47]

Habermas wants to integrate the struggle for power into the political. But as he sees the positive aspects of power as exclusively associated with communicative action, he ends up considering strategic action oriented towards gaining power as the source of a violence that represses communication:

> Be that as it may, we cannot exclude the element of strategic action from the concept of the political. We want to understand the violence exercised by way of strategic action as the capacity to keep other individuals or groups from perceiving their interests. In this sense, violence has always belonged to the means for acquiring and holding onto power.[48]

This violence exercised by strategic action is not, however, an open form of violence but a violence that knows how to present itself as legitimate power. Habermas calls it 'structural violence' – it erects 'communicative blocks' that go unnoticed:

Structural violence is not manifest *as violence*; instead it blocks in an unnoticed fashion those communications in which are shaped and propagated the convictions effective for legitimation ... it [i.e. the hypothesis of structural violence] can make plausible how convictions are formed by which the subjects deceive themselves about themselves and their situation ... In systematically restricted communications, the participants form convictions that are free from compulsion from a subjective point of view; thereby they communicatively engender a power, which, as soon as it is institutionalized, can also be turned against the participants.[49]

The idea of an action that is purely oriented towards reaching understanding, or of pure, undistorted communication, makes any social asymmetry appear as violence. The abstract idea of a power that is produced purely by communicative means cannot be given a 'realistic twist' by expanding it to include an *equally abstract* idea of a power that seems to be attached to strategic action. It is much more realistic to assume that communication is *always already* strategic. According to that idea, strategic action would not be the source of a specific 'violence' but a *constitutive element of power* which can therefore never be purely communicative or oriented towards reaching understanding.

Only with the assumption that communicative action is at the same time strategic is power given a 'realistic twist'. The result is a flexible concept of power that allows for different forms of power which emerge *on the basis of different internal structures of mediation*. From this perspective, asymmetric situations do not result from violence but from forms of power that lack mediation. Violence only signifies a particular constellation in which mediation is reduced to nothing. Because of this absence of mediation, violence deprives the participants in the communication of *any feeling of freedom*. A power constellation in which the party that is submitted to power fully accepts the domination of the other party does not represent a violent relationship even if it produces a pronounced asymmetry.

As opposed to violence, power does not exclude the possibility of a feeling of freedom. It even intentionally produces it in order to stabilize itself. The ideologies or narratives that provide legitimacy, which inscribe a fixed, asymmetric relationship through the channels of communication, should still be seen as situated at the level of power. Violence is never *narrative*. If there is any element of narration, which is after all always an attempt at mediation, we enter the realm of power.

Politics is more than a struggle for a power that has been turned into a material good that is positive in itself. In that sense, politics exceeds 'power politics'. But at the same time, politics is not exhausted by collective action as such. Rather, political practice in the emphatic sense is the active shaping or influencing of collective action,[50] a practice that, however, aims not only at communication oriented towards reaching understanding but also at the affirmation of interests and values. To the extent that political communication cannot be decoupled from strategic action, politics is always *power politics*. A being that is only oriented towards reaching understanding is an abstraction – not only in the case of politics but also in the case of anthropology and even ontology. Political action is constituted not by consensus but by *compromise* as the act of *balancing power*. *Compromittere* means: to leave the decision pertaining to a particular matter to the verdict of an arbiter. Thus, politics is a practice of *power and decision*.

5

The Ethics of Power

In *The Nomos of the Earth*, Carl Schmitt points out the legally constitutive force of the soil, the *'terrestrial'* origin of law.[1] He calls 'land-appropriation' the 'archetype of a constitutive legal process',[2] which 'constitutes the original spatial order, the source of all further concrete order and all further law'.[3] The appropriation of land thus opens up a legal *space as such*, turns the earth into a *location* [*Ort*]. Order, according to Schmitt, is *'orientation'* [*Ortung*].[4]

Heidegger, in *On the Way to Language*, also refers to *orientation*: 'Originally the word "site" [Ort] suggests a place in which everything comes together, is concentrated. The site gathers unto itself, supremely and in the extreme.'[5] The site founds an order, a *'nomos'*,[6] which bears and binds everything that *is*, and which gives it a hold [Halt], an abode [Aufenthalt]. In this process, the site sites without the use of violence. What is 'gathered' is not subjected to any coercion. Heidegger's site [Ort] is characterized by intense mediation. The site penetrates 'with its light all it has gathered, only thus releasing it into its own nature', bestowing on it what is its *own*.[7] The site therefore 'gathers in'[8] – 'supremely and in the extreme' – because it does not repress what is gathered but releases it 'into its own nature'.

Interestingly, Heidegger does not give further thought to the morphology of sites. The site refers to the *tip* of the *spear*.[9] The term '*tip*' means that sites are *centred*. A site 'gathers' everything 'into' *itself*. Thus, it is structured *ipsocentrically*. The tip of a spear is anything but *friendly*; violence and coercion may emanate from it. Heidegger does not consider this possibility of repression and domination. He only perceives the *tip* with regard to the possibility of a *highest mediation*. But if a site is very poor in terms of mediation, then the tip finds expression in coercion and repression.

Heidegger does not connect orientation with power.[10] The morphology of sites, however, makes it possible to interpret orientation as a process of power. A site 'gathers in', 'gathers unto *itself*'.[11] All forces meet in the tip, form a *continuum*. The fundamental trait [Zug] of the site is a pull towards *itself* [Zug zu *sich*]. Pulling or gathering everything unto itself, it forms an *ipsocentric continuum*. The pull towards *itself* and the formation of a continuum turn *orientation* into a process of power. That 'tip of the spear' in which 'everything comes together' points to the *ipseity* of a site that wills *itself*. Derrida is another thinker who recognizes that the idea of ipseity and that of power belong together: 'the idea of force (*kratos*), of power, and of mastery, is analytically included in the concept of ipseity'.[12] The sovereignty of a political site is also based on this ipseity. And property, the house (*oikos*), or capital depend on the ipseity of a site as well. Every power structure, it follows, is *ipsocentric*.

The process of globalization loosens the ties that bind power to territory. Transnational power structures that act like '*quasi-states*' are not bound to any particular territory.[13]

81

They are not *terrestrial*. They do not require 'land-appropriation' in the classical sense of the term in order to create or expand their power. However, globalization does not altogether undermine the logic of orientation. Orientation, after all, means the creation of an ipsocentrically organized *space* which pulls and gathers everything unto *itself*. Transnational power structures may have broken out of the 'cage of the territorial nation-state-organized power game', but they are not therefore *without a site*. They occupy new spaces which are, however, not tied to any national territories. Power cannot emerge in a *nowhere*. In the context of globalization, it is mainly deterritorialization that attracts attention. But globalization also generates various forms of *re-orientation* [*Re-Ortung*]. This is its dialectic.

In both the territorial domain and the 'digital *domain*', the process of power is an *orientation*.[14] Just as, in the global age, *space* is *opened up digitally*, for the most part, so orientation also takes place digitally. Thus, the formation and expansion of power needs a *digital land-appropriation*, a *digital reclamation of land*. Regarding the logic of power, there is no essential difference between *terrestrial* and *digital orientation*.[15] In the case of the latter, the one who conquers or dominates the digital space holds the power. The *market* is also a space that can be occupied through an *economic land-appropriation*. The battle over shares of the market is similar to the battle over *spaces*. The global market may no longer have any *terrestrial* ties, but it does not therefore render *orientation* superfluous. Rather, in the case of the global market, it is also important to position *oneself*, to establish an orientation for *oneself* [*sich zu verorten*]. 'Mergers' and 'take-overs' do not fundamentally differ from *land-appropriation*. They expand power.

The question of the *ethical dimension of power* arises in relation to its structure as a gathering. Power is centralizing. It gathers everything unto *itself* and unto the *one* centre [aufs

Eine]. If it realizes its pull towards the one in an absolute way, all that is adjacent to it [das Danebenliegende], the manifold, is *only* perceived as something to be *collected* and *appropriated*. The spaces which evade the one, or offer resistance, become off-sites [Ab-Orte] and are thus *de-sited* [*entortet*] or devalued.[16] The question is whether enough force, even *friendliness*, is immanent in power *as such* to make the off-sites *become sites again*.[17] Power certainly possesses the capacity of mediation. Thus, it does not fundamentally exclude freedom. But mediation *on the basis of power* has limits.

Power is *ipsocentric*. Ipseity is immanent to power as such. Every political or economic site strives towards *itself*, maintains *itself*. The will to *self* is always already contained in the concept of power. Without this ipsocentric striving, no power structure would ever emerge. The 'tip of the spear', in particular, points towards this ipseity that is immanent in any power structure.

The absoluteness of power consists in an *absolute immunity*, in an absolute inviolability of *self*. Thus, Derrida links the ethical dimension of power to a kind of 'autoimmunity' that leads to a moderation of ipseity.[18] Autoimmunity is meant to lead to an openness towards that 'alterity that is not reappropriable by the ipseity of a sovereign power and a calculable knowledge'.[19] However, Derrida's 'autoimmunity' is not without its problems. Were it to lead to total self-destruction, it would be an absolute evil. It would bring about an anomie, an anarchy, a total dissolution of the site or house (*oikos*). But *without a house* there can be no hospitality either. The ethical dimension of power requires, however, that a site exceed its ipsocentric striving, that it grant spaces, even residential spaces, not only to the *one* but also to the *manifold* and to that which *is adjacent*; it requires that it is affected by an originary friendliness which *slows down*, even *arrests* [*verhält*], this striving, this will to *self*. A different movement from that emanating from power emanates from friendliness. Power as such lacks the openness to alterity. It is inclined towards the *repetition of self and of the same*. Thus, the striving towards the repetition *of self* and the enlargement *of self* is also immanent to capital, which, like sites, moves towards the tip.[20]

The beginnings of an ethics of power can be found in Foucault, too. In the 1980s, he subscribed to a concept of power dominated by the idea of freedom. He was terse when confronted with the question of the ubiquity of power: 'I am sometimes asked: "But if power is everywhere, there is no freedom." I answer that if there are relations of power in every social field, this is because there is freedom everywhere.'[21] Foucault now tried to separate power relations from relations of domination or coercion by tying them closely to the notion of freedom. According to this approach, power relations do not only presuppose a pre-existing freedom because they emerge only out of its repression. Rather, freedom also represents an important, even the main, supporting element within power relations. Accordingly, power can only be exerted over 'free subjects'. And these subjects must remain free in order for the power relations to continue existing:

> Where the determining factors saturate the whole, there is no relationship of power; slavery is not a power relationship when man is in chains. (In this case it is a question of a physical relationship of constraint.) Consequently, there is no face-to-face confrontation of power and freedom, which are mutually exclusive (freedom disappears everywhere power is exercised), but a much more complicated interplay. In this game freedom may well appear as the condition for the exercise of power.[22]

Foucault's argument in this passage is not quite coherent. Slavery, even if the slave is in chains, remains after all a relation of power. The slave still has the option of saying 'no', i.e. refusing to obey his or her master even when faced with the threat of death. In that sense, the slave in chains is also free: he still has the *choice* between death and obedience. It is not only with the possibility of movement or escape that slavery becomes a power relation; the slave's 'yes' already turns it into one. The master, by contrast, loses his or her power the very moment that the slave categorically refuses to obey. For that to happen, it is immaterial whether the slave is in chains or has the possibility of fleeing. A minimal freedom, in this case the option of saying 'yes' or 'no', is the presupposition of a power relation. But it does not justify the assumption that power is a 'game'.

As opposed to pure violence, which does not allow for either a 'yes' or 'no', i.e. rules out any *choice* and turns the other into an absolutely passive thing,[23] a power relation contains the possibility of resistance in itself. 'No' is a form of resistance. Even if one is subjected to power and obeys the master absolutely and out of *free* choice, one has *in principle* the option of resistance. Power is the greatest, however, where the holder of power encounters no resistance whatsoever. There is no resistance not only in the case of infinite violence but also in the case of infinite power. Thus, there may well be a power relation without any resistance. Foucault apparently does not notice this constellation. He takes his cue from the paradigm of struggle, a struggle that takes the form of a contest:

> For, if it is true that at the heart of power relations and as a permanent condition of their existence there is an insubordination and a certain essential obstinacy on the part of the principles of freedom, then there is no relationship of power without the means of escape or possible flight[, without a possible reversal of the situation.][24]

85

According to Foucault's revised conception, the playful moment that is blocked by domination (because domination does not allow for openness or for a 'reversal of the situation') is immanent to power. However, this concept of domination is not without problems. Domination should not be strictly opposed to power relations. The condition of domination is one in which power relations gain stability. The *openness* of *games* is also not a trait of the essence of power. On the contrary, power *tends to reduce openness*. It is possible that the *fear* of openness and instability fuels the desire for more power. Power tries to solidify and to stabilize its position by eradicating spaces open to play, or incalculable spaces. Power spaces are strategic spaces. However, strategic openness is not identical with the pleasurable openness or uncertainty intrinsic to play.

By defining power as an 'open' game, or emphatically demanding 'practices of freedom', Foucault formulates a concept of power *in which, to a certain extent, a critique of power is already contained*. Power as an 'open-ended strategic game'[25] is, as Foucault himself points out, precisely not what 'people ordinarily call "power"'.[26] Foucault's revised concept of power results from an *ethos of freedom*, for the aim is 'to acquire the rules of law, the management techniques, and also the morality, the *ethos*, the practice of the self, that will allow us to play these games of power with as little domination as possible'.[27] Thus, an ethos of freedom stops power from solidifying into domination and makes sure that it remains an open game.

With regard to the logic of power, it cannot be disputed that power relations presuppose a minimal amount of freedom. One cannot enter into a power relation with a passive thing that does not offer any resistance. But Foucault uses the concept of 'freedom' in an emphatic sense. The freedom he connects to the processes of power far exceeds the minimal requirement that follows from the logic of power. He connects the processes of power with a 'practice of freedom' that presupposes a 'liberation' from an 'oppressive morality'.[28] There is an argumentative vagueness in Foucault's *silent transition from freedom as a structural presupposition of power relations to an ethics of freedom*. Foucault tacitly transforms freedom as a structural element of power relations into something *ethical*. But such an ethical quality does not inhere in power as such. With the help of this very fragile transition from the logic of power to the ethics of power, Foucault introduces a difference between power and domination.

Foucault's concept of power, which rests on 'practices of freedom', is too vague.[29] Apparently, he tries to bring power and freedom together. As opposed to Hegel, however, whose idea of 'free power' takes mediation and reconciliation as its points of orientation, Foucault consistently conceives of power processes as struggles, although he moderates or transforms them into open contests which lack the *tip of domination*. This allows him to keep power in a state of playful hovering. This is a very artificial concept of power. Thus, Foucault moves away from the real processes of power.

In the 1980s, Foucault's thought was dominated by the idea of freedom, and his revised concept of power is also affected by this emphasis on freedom. Ethics, Foucault says, is a 'practice of freedom', and '[f]reedom is the ontological condition of ethics'.[30] In this context, Foucault refers to the classical practice of care of the self, which, it is assumed, was concerned with 'liberation from what we do not control'[31] and with 'a perfect and complete relationship to the self',[32] i.e. with taking possession of oneself. This freedom-orientated care of the self implies care about the right way of using power. According to this ethics, the abuse of power results from having become 'the slave of one's desire'.[33] This leads to the loss of one's freedom, the 'enslavement of the self by oneself': 'The individual's attitude toward himself, the way in which he ensured his own freedom with regard to himself, and the form of supremacy he maintained over himself were a contributing element to the well-being and good order of the city.'[34] Taking Greco-Roman thought as his point of departure, Foucault connects the practice of care of the self with learning to make the right use of power. Accordingly, 'the risk of dominating others and exercising a tyrannical power over them arises precisely only when one has not taken care of the self and has become the slave of one's desires'.[35] Thus, the aim is 'to avoid the trap of tyrannical authority (over others) coupled with a soul tyrannized by desires'. Complete 'power over oneself' is the 'principle of internal regulation' of the exercise of political power. Thus, Foucault quotes Plato: 'The most kingly man was king of himself (*basilikos, basileuon heautou*).'[36]

What should be questioned in this argument is the assumption of a connection between exercising tyrannical power and a soul that is tyrannized by its desires. Complete self-control or 'power over oneself' does not rule out violent rule by definition. Further, care of the self can become thoroughly detached from care for others. The ultimate tie between care of the self and care of others rests solely on the calculation that, in the end, the well-being of others serves one's own well-being. Apart from the circularity inherent in such economic calculation [tauschökonomische Zirkularität],[37] the ethics of the self cannot include the other in the horizon of the self. We also need to distinguish between power and violence. 'Tyrannical power' is, in fact, a form of violence. It is, we should not forget, incapable of any *mediation*. Power, by contrast, must *include* others in order to nestle in their *souls* and make itself indestructible. Intrinsic to power is also a care for *mediation*. It is never blind. By contrast, tyranny, which is blind to mediation, destabilizes power.

Foucault raises care of the self to the status of an ethical principle and awards it preference over care for others: 'Care for others should not be put before the care of oneself. The Care of the self is ethically prior in that the relationship with oneself is ontologically prior.'[38] Do we therefore have to assume, without any further ado, a continuity between ethics and ontology? Does the difference between ethics and ontology not consist precisely in the fact that ethics *questions* the ontological preference of the relation to self? Does ethics in the emphatic sense not include an attempt at questioning the very ontology which assigns the greatest importance to the relation to self?

Foucault's ethics of power is based on an ethics of care of the self. Due to its orientation towards the self, it is unable to open up those spaces that transcend the intentionality of power, i.e. the return to the *self*.[39] Power is itself, after all, a phenomenon of the self or subjectivity. Foucault's ethics of power is not open to the *other of power* which would create a trait that runs counter to the return to the *self*. It also fails to generate the friendliness that makes visible what does not appear within the *economy* of care of the self.

It is interesting that Foucault holds on to the paradigm of possession of self. He apparently feels committed to that European cultural tradition which is formed by 'a series of difficult attempts, to reconstitute an ethics and an aesthetics of the self'.[40] According to Foucault, this tradition includes – apart from Montaigne, Baudelaire and Schopenhauer – Nietzsche, whose philosophy of power exhibits certain traits of an ethics and aesthetics of the self while at the same time developing a dynamic, or dialectic, which leads power beyond itself.

'Let us be honest with ourselves to this extent at least!' Nietzsche exclaims.[41] Life, he says, 'is *essentially* a process of appropriating, injuring, overpowering the alien and the weaker, oppressing, being harsh, imposing your own form, incorporating, and at least, in its mildest form, exploiting'.[42] For Nietzsche, exploitation 'does not belong to a corrupted or imperfect, primitive society'. Rather, 'as a fundamental organic function', it is part of 'the *essence* of being alive'. It is a 'result of genuine will to power, which is just the will of life'.[43] Every living body, he says, wants to 'grow, spread, grab, win dominance', and 'not out of any morality or immorality, but because it is *alive*, and because life *is* precisely will to power'.[44]

Here, the exercise of power means to impose *oneself* on the other, to outgrow, overgrow the other, so to speak, i.e. to *continue oneself* in the other or to spread a continuity – a *continuum of self* – throughout the other. Willing-*oneself* is a property peculiar to power. Power by itself would never be able to produce a counter-trait to this intentionality of willing-*oneself*, to bring about any turn towards the other that is not at the same time a return to *itself*, hence no care for the other that exceeds care of the *self*. Power is tied to this constant self-reference and self-indulgence, to this permanent return to itself: 'Feeling of power, first conquering, then dominating (organizing) – it regulates what it has overcome for the purpose of *its* preservation and *to that purpose it preserves what it has overcome.*'[45]

Nietzsche does not limit the range of power to human conduct. Rather, he elevates it to the status of a principle of life as such. Mono-cellular organisms already strive for power: 'Let us consider the simplest case, that of primitive nutrition: the protoplasm extends its pseudopodia in order to search for something that offers resistance – not because of hunger, but because of the will to power.'[46] Even truth is interpreted as a process of power: it is the perspective of the powerful, which the powerful inoculates into the others, thus continuing him- or herself in them. Truth is a medium of power. The beautiful also follows the economy of power: 'Ruthless development of forms: the most beautiful are only the strongest: as the ones that are victorious they maintain themselves and enjoy their type, procreation.'[47] Power secures the continuation of a type. Thus, it creates a continuity. Philosophers, too, strive to extend their perspectives and thus to continue *themselves*. This is how Nietzsche interprets Plato's belief 'that even philosophy is a kind of sublimated sexual and procreational drive'.[48]

'Conquest', 'exploitation' or 'injury' thus belong to the 'essence of being alive'. They reflect the will to power, which animates life. Everything that is alive wants to grow, grab and appropriate. In light of this general, omnipotent will to power, there arises the difficult question of the origin of this 'aversion [Widerwille] against what is all-too alive', an aversion which characterizes 'the *serenity* of strong souls'.[49] Nietzsche apparently thinks that power is not exhausted by the negative forms of exploitation or repression. Rather, he fuses it with other qualities, which radically changes its character. Thus, he speaks of 'justice' as a 'function of a power with a vast vision'.[50] Exploitative or repressive power may certainly also have vast vision. But as long as it remains ipsocentric, that vast vision ultimately only serves the purposes of the self, because it only looks for things that may expand the circle of the self. Power can only extend its vision *for the sake of the vastness and the things that populate this vastness if it is touched by something that is not power, that is not circling around the self.* Justice, with its 'lofty, clear objectivity both penetrating and merciful',[51] is therefore not an effect of power alone. It 'observes carefully from all sides',[52] attends to what is small and fleeting as well, with an eye that is not the eye of power. Power is ignorant of that '*most tender* emotion' of friendliness with a mild gaze.[53] Only an *extrinsic* quality that cannot be attributed to power can possibly enable it to develop a vast, far-reaching, friendly gaze.

When we look at it more carefully, we can see that justice creates a movement that is opposed to the gathering structure of power. For in power there inheres the *trait* of being pulled *towards the one*, and thus there emerges from it no friendliness towards plurality, the manifold, the diverse, what is adjacent, or what drifts off. Justice, by contrast, 'wants to give to each his own, whether the thing be dead or living, real or imaginary'.[54] Hence, it is neither ipsocentric nor *centric* in any other way. Nietzsche also calls it 'an opponent of convictions'.[55] The just person listens to the things rather than to *him- or herself*. To refrain from having convictions means at the same time to refrain from *oneself*. The aim is – for the benefit of the things – to hear more, to see more, to go beyond one's momentary convictions, which always contain a being-convinced-of-oneself. The just person reserves his or her judgement, which would *always* be *too early*. A judgement would already be a betrayal of the other: '*Rare abstemiousness* – It is often no small sign of humanity not to wish to judge another and to refrain from thinking about him.'[56] Justice is practised by suspending one's convictions, one's opinions about the other, by *hearing*, *listening*, by refraining from judgements, i.e. from *oneself*. For the self enters the scene *always too early* and to the disadvantage of the other. Such singular abstinence cannot originate from power as such. There is no *hesitation* to be found in power. Power as such never refuses to judge or to think about the other. Rather, it is made up of judgements and convictions.

Only 'power with a vast vision', i.e. the power with an eye that 'observes carefully from all sides', is capable of *orientating* [kann *orten*] without producing off-sites [Ab-Orte]. Thus, it founds *just* sites that give 'to each his own'. Nietzsche does not stop at this justice. He apparently has in mind a limitless friendliness which welcomes all and sundry without distinction: 'everything becoming, roaming, seeking, fleeing shall be welcomed by me at this place! From now on, hospitality [Gastfreundschaft] shall be the only friendship [Freundschaft] I know.'[57] This singular kind of hospitality gives 'to each' *more than his own*. This is the difference between a *site of hospitality* and a just site. Heidegger's site is also a just site in so far as it penetrates 'with its light all it has gathered, only thus releasing it into *its* own nature'. But it cannot develop a limitless hospitality that welcomes and affirms what lies outside its gathering.

In *Daybreak*, Nietzsche juxtaposes the Christian maxim to love thy neighbour with an aristocratic friendliness:

> *A different kind of neighbour-love.* – Behaviour that is excited, noisy, inconsistent, nervous constitutes the antithesis of *great passion*: the latter, dwelling within like a dark fire and there assembling all that is hot and ardent, leaves a man looking outwardly cold and indifferent and impresses upon his features a certain impassivity. Such men are, to be sure, occasionally capable of *neighbour-love* – but it is a kind different from that of the sociable and anxious to please: it is a *gentle, reflective, relaxed friendliness* [emph. B.-Ch. H.]; it is as though they were gazing out of the windows of their castle, which is their fortress and for that reason also their prison – to gaze into what is strange and free, into *what is different*, does them so much good![58]

This aristocratic friendliness,[59] in which the self is still a prisoner of itself, is expanded by Nietzsche into an unconditional hospitality which knows no 'impassibility', no castle or fortress of the self. He speaks of a 'dangerous carelessness', of a 'carelessness of the overly rich soul which never *made efforts* at making friends, but rather only knows of hospitality, only ever practices hospitality and knows how to practice it – heart and house open to anyone who wants to enter, whether they be beggars, or cripples, or kings'.[60] This unconditional hospitality is opposed to that kind of friendship which sees in a friend only 'another self'.[61] The latter is a 'dangerous carelessness' because it is not a *practice of care of the self*, because it never takes care of the self.

On the basis of the economy of ipsocentric power, it cannot be explained why that gaze at what is strange, at the other, does the powerful Lord of the castle so much good. This gaze is not fuelled by the intention of conquering. Just as little can we explain why the powerful experience their own castles as a prison. What causes them to look away from themselves and into the other, to open their gaze unreservedly towards the strange? What causes the powerful to go beyond aristocratic friendliness and adopt an indiscriminate, unconditional, asymmetric friendliness?[62] How could an ipsocentric power create all this friendliness, this for-the-other, out of itself?

Ultimately – and this is problematic – Nietzsche derives friendliness from power, namely from 'power that wants to overflow'.[63] Generosity is an 'impulse generated by the over-abundance of power'.[64] Accordingly, the ipsocentric character of power is not called into question. The essential trait of this morality of the powerful is precisely 'self-aggrandisement'.[65] But can this 'awareness of a wealth that wants to give away and share' really be based on 'self-aggrandisement'? The intentionality that is its foundation would re-appropriate anything it had given away. The powerful likes *him- or herself* when giving, taking it as an expression of his or her power. Mercy, in this sense, is the highest affirmation of power and of the self of the powerful. In giving, the powerful enjoys *him- or herself*. Yet this enjoyment of self makes that 'overflowing' [Überströmen] impossible, as such overflowing would *flood* the self. It is the impossibility of a return to self that characterizes this *over* [dieses *Über*].

Nietzsche further juxtaposes the 'rabble' and 'despotic

rule' to what is noble: 'Therefore, my brothers, we need a *new nobility*, which is the adversary of all rabble and all despotic rule and which writes anew the word "noble" on new tablets.'[66] In this passage, Nietzsche distinguishes between noble power and power as despotic rule. However, this distinction presupposes that it is not power as such that is noble. That the powerful shed the vulgarity of the rabble and assume an aura of noblesse is not because of power. Power, *in itself*, does not have the ability to soar to the level of 'abundance' that characterizes the noble person. Due to the *desire* that inheres in power, it will never be able to bring about a 'feeling of plenty'. Plentifulness or over-abundance does not result simply from the accumulation of power. Perhaps power is never free from a feeling of lack.

Power by itself, even under conditions of 'over-abundance', does not let the soul drift off into that 'dangerous carelessness' which 'only knows of hospitality'. Because of its ipsocentric nature, it is not capable of that boundless hospitality which opens its house to 'anyone'. Nietzsche knows very well what a hospitality that follows the economy of the self looks like:

> *Hospitality.* – The meaning of the usages of hospitality is the paralysing of enmity in the stranger. Where the stranger is no longer felt to be first and foremost an enemy, hospitality decreases; it flourishes as long as its evil presupposition flourishes.[67]

Friendliness is not a property intrinsic to power. Rather, power has to be *touched by something that is not part of itself* in order to be able *to mediate beyond the means of its own capacity for mediation*. Friendliness is also a type of mediation, even an intense form of mediation. But it lacks the intentionality of power, namely the 'tip' of *subjectivity*. The *friendly site* differs from the site of power in that it does not perceive what is isolated, or *what is adjacent*, exclusively from the perspective of the continuity of the one, but also lets it shine in its *suchness*. Friendliness orientates [verortet] beyond orientation based on power. Thus, it does not create any off-sites [Ab-Ort]. It counteracts the *de-siting* [*Entortung*] from which power is never entirely safe.

Even where power in its 'over-abundance' expresses itself as unconditional 'hospitality', it borders on the *other of power*. It has then become a kind of *over*-power which contains a singular *self-suspension of power* within itself. From it emanates that limitless giving which cannot be re-appropriated by the return to *oneself*, by the willing of *oneself* – a giving that *takes place*, so to speak, *unconsciously and without intention*, a boundless friendliness that *precedes* any care for the other, *precedes* any emphatic for-the-other.

Nietzsche, this unusual philosopher of the 'will to power', deserves to be listened to very carefully when he invokes the other of power and the will:

> Outside the windows, there lies the autumn, full of thoughts, in a clear and mild sunlight; the autumn of the North which I love as much as my very best friends because it is so mature and unconsciously without a wish. A fruit falls off a tree, without help from the wind. ... in perfect silence, and happy, it falls down. It does not desire anything for itself and it gives everything of itself.[68]

What is invoked in this passage is a *here* that is unconsciously without a wish, even selfless, without a *name*[69] and without desire. Nietzsche's philosophy of the 'will to power', which, according to Foucault, is an 'ethics and aesthetics of the self', leads to a *nemology*, to an ethics and aesthetics of the *no one*, a *friendliness* free of intentions, even free of *wishes*.[70] Nietzsche must have heard this divine voice again and again, a divine voice which called on him to give *himself* away, to empty *himself* and thus become a *no one*:

> You would like to give away your excess,
> but you are yourself this excess!
> Be clever, you rich one!
> *Give yourself away first*, oh, Zarathustra![71]

NOTES

Preface

1 See Luhmann, 'Klassische Theorie der Macht: Kritik ihrer Prämissen', p. 149.

1 The Logic of Power

1 Ulrich Beck rightly remarks that *'there is a positive correlation between the taken-for-grantedness of power, the forgetting of power, and the dimensions of power.* One could almost say that, wherever nobody is talking about power, that is where it unquestionably exists, at once secure and great in its unquestionability. Wherever power is the subject of discussion, that is the start of its decline.' Beck, *Power in the Global Age*, p. 57.

2 Luhmann, 'Power', p. 124: 'In fact ... the existence of a power differential and the anticipation of a power-based decision make it quite senseless for the subordinate even to make up his mind. And it is precisely in this that the function of power lies. It secures possible chains of effect independent of the will of the participant who is subjected to power – whether he wishes

it or not. The causality of power lies in neutralizing the will, but not necessarily in breaking the will of the inferior. It also affects him, and that most precisely, when he intended to do that same thing and then learns that he has to do it anyway.'

3 If, by contrast, power is identified with coercion and repression, it will be interpreted as the capacity to say 'No'. This fails to recognize that 'Yes' is actually the expression of a higher power. 'Yes' does not need to be the result of powerlessness. See Sofsky and Paris, *Figurationen sozialer Macht*, p. 9: 'A society without power would be a society of yes-sayers. Whoever wants to abolish power would have to deprive everyone of the capacity to say "No". Because the actions of one person come to an end through the resistance of another, through this other's irremovable independence and freedom to do something else but what is expected of him or her. This is what power attacks. It expands the freedom of the one at the expense of the other by breaking the "No", by negating the freedom, of the latter. Power is the freedom to destroy freedom.'

4 Transl. note: The German word 'Gewalt' can mean an authority, a form of physical or non-physical violence, or a power.

5 Transl. note: The German formulation 'die *Macht* ... zu *machen*' hints at a connection between power and making, producing, creating.

6 See Kantorowicz, *The King's Two Bodies*.

7 Luhmann, 'Power', p. 125.

8 Luhmann, 'Macht und System', p. 476.

9 See Luhmann, 'Power', pp. 125f.: 'Only when, and in so far as, goods are scarce does the active claim to some of them on the part of one person become a problem for others, and this situation is then regulated by a communication medium, which transfers the action selected by the one person into the experience of the others and so makes it acceptable.'

10 Weber, *Economy and Society*, p. 53.

11 Luhmann, *Soziologische Aufklärung 4*, p. 117.
12 Luhmann, 'Macht und System', p. 476. See ibid.: 'The threat of direct confrontation or physical violence is a very efficient instrument of power in so far as it is context-independent. But in the case of complex processes it is too coarse. A system that only knows violence as an instrument of power is poor in differentiation and only capable of little productivity. A complex system is dependent on subtly structured steering and power mechanisms. Mere muscle power is of little help here. In a complex system, constellations emerge in which indirect, less obvious instruments of power are far more efficient than the threat of violence.'
13 Luhmann, *Soziologische Aufklärung 4*, p. 119.
14 Luhmann, 'Power', p. 123.
15 Luhmann, 'Klassische Theorie der Macht: Kritik ihrer Prämissen', p. 163.
16 Likert, *Neue Ansätze der Unternehmensführung*, p. 63.
17 Luhmann, 'Macht und System', p. 477.
18 See Foucault, *The History of Sexuality, Vol. 1*, p. 144.
19 According to Weber, the bureaucratization and anonymization of an organization lead to the development of a form of power the effects of which are entirely without 'charisma'. Genuinely charismatic authority [charismatische Herrschaft] does not require any authorities, civil servants or regulations. It needs no officials or spheres of competence. Weber juxtaposes it with 'bureaucratic authority' [bürokratische Herrschaft], which is bound up with rules that can be discursively analysed. See Weber, *Economy and Society*, pp. 243f. Because rules are alien to it, charismatic rule radically reduces complexity. This probably explains its seductive power. For all charismatic rule, Weber says, the proposition holds: 'It is written ... but I say unto you' (ibid., p. 978).
20 Luhmann, 'Macht und System', p. 479.
21 Ibid., p. 480.

22 Ibid.

23 Ibid., p. 481.

24 Ibid.

25 Transl. note: '*sich* in Alter zu *kontinuieren*'. The formulation points towards the fundamental idea of the continuum.

26 Paul Tillich is among those who draw attention to the need for a comprehensive sphere of power that allows for supranational action. See Tillich, 'Das Problem der Macht: Versuch einer philosophischen Grundlegung', p. 203: 'The last remaining comprehensive groups that create positions of power in order to realize their social being are at present the nation states, whose main representatives are characterized as "powers", i.e. as the most comprehensive bearers of social being. Sovereignty is a characteristic of a power group that is no longer integrated into a more comprehensive group. Any encounter then takes place under conditions of an unstable balance that permanently enters into new constellations. As there is no acknowledged position of power, the arbitrary threat and use of violence is the only method for establishing one's power. This situation can only be changed by creating a comprehensive position of power that is acknowledged and legally binding, i.e. by creating unity in a supranational state which overcomes individual sovereignty.'

27 The terror of the concentration camps certainly is based on this naked violence. The term 'absolute power', which Wolfgang Sofsky uses to characterize the terror of the concentration camps, is not fitting. Absolute power presupposes some communicative mediation, which is entirely absent from naked violence. See Sofsky, *The Order of Terror*. For Hegel, 'absolute power' is anything but the violence of terror: 'Absolute power does not rule; in ruling the other vanishes – here it stays, but obeys, serves as a means.' See Hegel, *Vorlesungen über die Philosophie der Religion I*, in *Werke*, vol. 16, p. 416.

28 Canetti, *Crowds and Power*, p. 251.

29 Ibid., p. 281.

30 Transl. note: 'Zeit-Raum'. Without the, unusual, hyphenation the composite noun would refer to a distinct 'space of time', an 'interval'.

2 The Semantics of Power

1 Nietzsche, *Nachgelassene Fragmente 1882–1884*, in *Sämtliche Werke: Kritische Studienausgabe* (hereafter KSA), vol. 10, p. 298. This is one of the passages which illustrate Nietzsche's rhetorical intensity particularly well. The well-known story of the 'muselmann', the inmate of a camp, demonstrates in frightening fashion the possibility of a language that is reduced to a *pure*, even *absolute*, giving of orders. The 'muselmann', it is said, was unable to distinguish between the biting cold and the order of the concentration camp guards. The word of the other, in this case, is experienced by the body literally as a sting or a painful bite. This proximity between physical pain and the word forcefully points to the *possibility of a language that hurts*.

2 Nietzsche, *On the Genealogy of Morality*, p. 12.

3 Nietzsche, *Nachgelassene Fragmente 1885–1887*, KSA 12, p. 142.

4 Nietzsche, *Beyond Good and Evil*, p. 106.

5 Nietzsche, *Nachgelassene Fragmente 1885–1887*, KSA 12, p. 97.

6 Nietzsche, *Nachgelassene Fragmente 1884–1885*, KSA 11, p. 699.

7 Nietzsche, *Nachgelassene Fragmente 1885–1887*, KSA 12, p. 114.

8 Nietzsche, *Nachgelassene Fragmente 1885–1887*, KSA 13, p. 44.

9 Nietzsche, *On the Genealogy of Morality*, p. 51.

10 Nietzsche, *Nachgelassene Fragmente 1885–1887*, KSA 12, p. 140.

11 Nietzsche, *Nachgelassene Fragmente 1885–1887*, KSA 9, p. 637.

12 Nietzsche, *Twilight of the Idols*, p. 197.

13 In his *Reflections on History*, p. 139, Burckhardt writes: 'Now power is of its nature evil, whoever wields it. It is not stability but a lust, and ipso facto insatiable, therefore unhappy in itself and doomed to make others unhappy.' Carl Schmitt remarks that the holders of power, who, according to Burckhardt, display the evil face of power, are all modern holders of power, and that the thesis of power as evil only began to spread in the nineteenth century. He therefore suspects that this condemnation of power is the result of power becoming something purely human. See Schmitt, *Dialogues on Power and Space*, p. 43. The de-theologization or secularization of power takes away its aura of the divine or of divine legitimation. This historical context gives Nietzsche's philosophy of the 'will to power' a specific significance. Nietzsche re-establishes power's dignity, so to speak, by elevating it to the status of a universal principle. The sacred 'earth' gives it back a divine expanse. The early Nietzsche, by contrast, did not yet have a positive concept of power. Rather, he followed Burckhardt's thesis of power as evil, if only formally, because even then Nietzsche integrated the power that is 'of its nature evil' into the process that gives rise to the arts and culture. It is a necessary evil that is similar to the 'spirit that eats away at the liver of the Promethean supporter of culture'. Thus, the arts and culture flourish on 'terrifying grounds'. According to this theory of culture, power is not directly or positively involved in the formation of culture and the arts. But it is its negative fomenter, so to speak. See Nietzsche, *Nachgelassene Schriften 1870–1873*, KSA 1, p. 767.

14 Foucault, *The History of Sexuality, Vol. 1*, p. 86.

15 See Fink-Eitel, *Foucault zur Einführung*, p. 115. Agamben is another author who perceives power as discussed by Foucault only from its negative side. Agamben takes away the positivity of power to which Foucault points repeatedly in his analyses, and has 'bio-power' (*Homo Sacer*, p. 3) – which, according

to Foucault, is not based on the threat of death but on the administration and organization of life – coincide with that power which brings about a life with 'an unconditional capacity to be killed' (p. 85), a bare and *naked* life, devoid of any legal mediation, i.e. *homo sacer*. Foucault, by contrast, takes 'bio-power' to be the process that steers *life* through norms and normalization, and that *also* means structuring life and *furnishing* it with sense. Bio-power does not equal exclusion and ban; rather it is designed as administration and organization. Axel Honneth, who mainly conceives of power as related to class struggles, is yet another example of an author to whom the positivity, or productivity, of power remains hidden. That is also the reason why, strangely, he does *not* touch upon the theory of 'communicative power' when discussing Habermas's work. 'Communicative power' is positive in so far as it is the foundation for acting together and action coordination. See Honneth, *The Critique of Power*.

16 Foucault, *Society Must be Defended*, p. 15. In a certain sense, Foucault is himself a victim of this prejudice. For Hegel, power is anything but repression. He was the first to coin the term 'free power'. The specificity of Hegel's theory of power is precisely the close association of power and freedom.

17 Foucault, *Discipline and Punish*, p. 194.

18 Foucault, *The History of Sexuality, Vol. 1*, p. 136.

19 Foucault, 'Truth and Power', p. 61.

20 Foucault, 'The History of Sexuality', p. 184.

21 Foucault, *Discipline and Punish*, p. 30.

22 The *soul* is more than just an 'effect and instrument of a political anatomy'. That *animation* (*psychisme* or *inspiration*) that Levinas uses in order to name an entirely different form of *subjugation*, namely the 'exposure to the other, the passivity of the for-the-other', which would be a counter-figure to the activity of power or domination, remains beyond Foucault's scope. See Levinas, *Otherwise than Being, or, Beyond Essence*, p. 71.

104

23 Foucault, *The History of Sexuality, Vol. 1*, p. 32.

24 Transl. note: The existing English translation renders this expression as 'deployment of sexuality'. I have here substituted the now more common form.

25 Ibid., p. 46.

26 Ibid., p. 44.

27 Ibid., p. 45.

28 Ibid., p. 86.

29 Foucault, 'Power and Norm: Notes', p. 59.

30 Foucault, *The History of Sexuality, Vol. 1*, p. 92.

31 Foucault, *Discipline and Punish*, p. 131.

32 Foucault, *The History of Sexuality, Vol. 1*, p. 148.

33 Ibid., p. 147.

34 Foucault, *Discipline and Punish*, p. 34 (emph. B.-Ch. H.).

35 Ibid., p. 101.

36 Ibid., pp. 102f. All educators and poets therefore make use of this pen and become moralists or missionaries of 'eternal reason': 'Filled with these terrible images and salutary ideas, each citizen will spread them through his family and there, by long accounts delivered with as much fervour as they are avidly listened to, his children gathered around him, will open up their young memories to receive, in imperishable lineaments, the notion of crime and punishment, the love of law and country, the respect and trust of the magistrature' (Servan, quoted ibid., p. 112).

37 Ibid., p. 128.

38 Ibid., p. 113 (transl. mod.).

39 Ibid., p. 307.

40 Ibid., p. 129.

41 Ibid., p. 130.

42 Ibid., p. 137.

43 Foucault, 'Power and Norm: Notes', p. 66.

44 Ibid., p. 135.

45 Ibid., p. 27.

46 Ibid., p. 137.

47 Transl. note: The German text plays on 'be-', the prefix of both verbs, which suggests work or writing being applied *to* or *on* the body.

48 Foucault draws attention to the historical significance of the body as such: 'But the body is also directly involved in a political field; power relations have an immediate hold upon it; they invest it, mark it, train it, torture it, force it to carry out tasks, to perform ceremonies, to emit signs' (ibid., p. 25).

49 Ibid., p. 65.

50 Ibid., p. 66. The term 'wily' suggests an actor or a subject with negative intentions that can be located, both problematic assumptions.

51 See Bourdieu, *Satz und Gegensatz*, p. 43: 'Political obedience is reflected in habitus, in the folds, in bodily habits, as well as in the automatisms of the brain.' [Transl. note: In the absence of an existing English translation of this text, I translate from the German text used by Han.]

52 Bourdieu, *Distinction*, p. 173.

53 Bourdieu, 'Eine sanfte Gewalt', p. 162. [Transl. note: In the absence of an existing English translation of this text, I translate from the German text used by Han.]

54 Bourdieu, *Satz und Gegensatz*, p. 43: 'The better person, for instance, as the Latin tells us, is a *nobilis*, someone who is a "known", an "acknowledged" person. However, as soon as you move outside the physicalism of relations between forces and try to introduce symbolic relations of knowledge, chances are that you revert back to the philosophical tradition of the subject and of consciousness and imagine these acts of acknowledgment as free acts of submission and of secret agreement. But neither sense nor knowledge implies consciousness ... The social actors, including those who are dominated, are affiliated with the social world (no matter how despicable and appalling this world may be) by a silently accepted complic-

ity. This complicity has the effect that certain aspects of this world always remain beyond critical questioning.'

55 Bourdieu, *The Logic of Practice*, p. 69.
56 Although Bourdieu read Heidegger intensely, he did not see the possibility of reading Heidegger's phenomenology of everydayness in terms of the logic of power.
57 Heidegger, *Being and Time*, p. 213.
58 Ibid., p. 211.
59 Ibid., p. 165.
60 Ibid., p. 164.
61 Ibid., p. 165.
62 Ibid.
63 Ibid., p. 167.
64 Ibid., p. 213.
65 Ibid., p. 165.
66 Transl. note: The translators speak of a 'levelling down' because Heidegger, in this passage, actually speaks of the suppression of any 'Vorrang', rendered as 'priority', rather than 'deviation'. In the background is Nietzsche's argument regarding the resentment of the masses against those who are noble.
67 Ibid., p. 164.
68 Ibid.
69 Ibid., p. 178. Bourdieu does not relate the 'they' to power. But he points out that moods have the character of a habitus. Moods, according to Bourdieu, remain 'irreducible to all objectification in speech or in any other form of expression'. Bourdieu, *The Political Ontology of Martin Heidegger*, p. 9.
70 Ibid., pp. 165f.
71 Foucault, *Mikrophysik der Macht*, p. 109. [Transl. note: In the absence of an existing English translation of this text, I translate from the German text used by Han.]
72 Heidegger, *Being and Time*, p. 164.
73 See ibid., p. 165.

74 Ibid., p. 224.

75 Ibid., p. 346.

76 Ibid., p. 187.

77 Ibid., p. 165.

3 The Metaphysics of Power

1 Foucault, 'The Ethics of the Concern for Self as a Practice of Freedom', p. 298. It is truly remarkable that, particularly in the 1980s, Foucault began to talk about freedom in the context of power. Neither *Discipline and Punish* nor the *Will to Knowledge* talked about freedom.

2 Heidegger, *The Will to Power as Art, Vols I and II*, p. 60.

3 Ibid., p. 61.

4 Ibid.

5 Transl. note: This neologism combines two meanings, 'going together with itself' and 'coming together with itself'.

6 Tillich, 'Das Problem der Macht', p. 203

7 Nietzsche, *Nachgelassene Fragmente 1875–1879*, KSA 8, p. 425.

8 Nietzsche, *Nachgelassene Fragmente 1882–1884*, KSA 10, p. 278.

9 Nietzsche, *Beyond Good and Evil*, p. 153.

10 Ibid.

11 Hegel, *Encyclopedia of the Philosophical Sciences in Outline, Part I: Science of Logic*, p. 289.

12 Hegel, *Hegel's Philosophy of Nature*, p. 397.

13 Hegel, *Enzyklopädie der philosophischen Wissenschaften: Dritter Teil: Die Philosophie des Geistes mit den mündlichen Zusätzen*, p. 21.

14 Hegel, *Lectures on the Philosophy of History*, p. 294 (transl. mod.).

15 Hegel, *Hegel's Philosophy of Nature*, p. 399.

16 Hegel, *Enzyklopädie der philosophischen Wissenschaften: Dritter Teil: Die Philosophie des Geistes mit den mündlichen Zusätzen*, p. 256.

17 Ibid.

18 Ibid., p. 22.

19 Transl. note: A literal translation of the German 'erinnern', 'to remember' or 'to recollect', would be 'to bring inside'.

20 Ibid., p. 244.

21 Ibid., p. 289.

22 Hegel, *Lectures on the Philosophy of History*, p. 395.

23 Tillich, 'Philosophie der Macht', p. 223. [Transl. note: These two lectures have not been translated, but the interested reader might want to consult Tillich, *Love, Power, and Justice*.]

24 Luhmann, *Soziologische Aufklärung 1*, pp. 38f.

25 Tillich, 'Philosophie der Macht', p. 209.

26 Ibid.

27 Hegel, *The Phenomenology of Spirit*, p. 19.

28 Hegel, *Lectures on the Philosophy of History*, p. 395.

29 Hegel, *Aesthetics: Lectures on Fine Art, Vol. I*, p. 110.

30 Hegel, *The Science of Logic II*, p. 532. [Transl. note: 'reaches out and embraces' translates 'übergreifen', which today evokes far more negative connotations; the nominalized form, 'Übergriff', denotes 'encroachment', 'assault' and 'abuse', including assault and abuse of a sexual nature.]

31 Foucault, *Discipline and Punish*, p. 30. [Transl. note: The full sentence runs: 'The man described for us, whom we are invited to free, is already in himself the effect of a subjection much more profound than himself.' I have retained the male gender in this case.]

32 Hegel, *Vorlesungen über die Philosophie der Religion II*, p. 55.

33 Hegel, *Berliner Schriften 1822–1831*, p. 373.

34 Hegel, *Vorlesungen über die Philosophie der Religion I*, p. 373.

35 Bataille, *Theory of Religion*, p. 49.

36 Ibid., p. 44.

37 Gerd Bergfleth in Bataille, *Theorie der Religion*, p. 145.

38 Bataille, *Theory of Religion*, p. 53 (transl. mod.).

39 Ibid., p. 19.

40 We may safely assume that this image is based on a projection of the human desire [Wunschbild] onto the 'animal'. That animal is as imaginary as the 'human being'.

41 Bataille, *Theory of Religion*, p. 18.

42 Ibid., p. 17.

43 Handke, 'Essay on Tiredness', p. 41 (transl. mod.). [Transl. note: The English translation opts for a free translation of this passage, rendering it as 'Tiredness is greater than the self.']

44 Deep tiredness is anything but consuming. The bright 'light of tiredness' (ibid., p. 28; transl. mod.) retains forms. It 'structures'. The tiredness is a 'clear-sighted tiredness' (ibid., p. 31). This also makes it friendly.

45 Ibid., p. 38.

46 Transl. note: The German is 'Gelassenheit' which, if read as the Heideggerian term, is usually translated as 'releasement'.

47 Ibid., p. 19 (transl. mod.). [Transl. note: Handke's remark concerns a group of workers. Hence, the English translation correctly gives: 'I had the impression that none of these workers dominated or commanded.']

48 Ibid., p. 41 (transl. mod.).

49 Hegel, *Vorlesungen über die Philosophie der Religion II*, p. 316.

50 Handke, 'Essay on Tiredness', p. 41. [Transl. note: Handke's actual words are: 'I conceive of the Pentecostal company that received the Holy Ghost as tired to a man.' The sentence is part of what he calls, in the same place, a 'Pindaric ode, not to a victor but to a tired man'.]

51 Ibid., p. 37.

52 Ibid., p. 43.

4 The Politics of Power

1 Schmitt, *Political Theology*, p. 5.

2 Ibid., p. 12.

3 Ibid., p. 15.

4 Ibid.

5   Hegel, *Elements of the Philosophy of Right*, p. 323.
6   Ibid., p. 316.
7   Ibid., p. 317.
8   Ibid., p. 321.
9   Ibid., p. 318.
10 Schmitt, *Dialogues on Power and Space*, pp. 34f.
11 Ibid., p. 37.
12 Ibid., p. 35.
13 Ibid., p. 46 (transl. mod.).
14 Ibid., p. 47. According to Schmitt, the Leviathan is 'a Super-Human [*Über-Mensch*] compiled of humans gathered together, which comes into existence via human consensus and yet, in the moment that it is present, exceeds all human consensus' (ibid., p. 46). It is the 'machine of machines' because it is the 'concrete presupposition of all further technological machines'. According to this idea, the Leviathan and modern technology have the same origin. They are both expressions of the 'Super-Power [*Über-Macht*]' (ibid.), which is stronger than any human 'will to power' (ibid., p. 47). Schmitt speaks of the 'power of the modern means of annihilation', which 'exceeds the force of the human individuals who invent those means and who bring them to be deployed as much as the capacities of modern machines and techniques exceed the force of human muscles and brains' (ibid., p. 45). It is problematic that Schmitt hypostasizes modern technology into a power with human beings at its mercy. Thus, in the face of this human impotence, he invokes the *human being*. The elevation of technology to the status of a super-power, however, conceals the actual truth, i.e. that technology is the means of power used by humans to extend *themselves* into the external world. Technologies extend human perception, the human body and even human habits into the world. In this way, they make the world over in the image of the human being. The Leviathan and technological gadgets

clearly resemble the human being. Thus, the human being can remain with *itself* in the world. This reduces the danger of self-alienation. Everywhere the human being returns to itself. In everything the human being sees itself. Technology produces the being-with-oneself-in-the-other, a space into which the human being can *continue itself*. When Heidegger, like Schmitt, elevates technology and turns it into a super-human power, he fails to see that technology bears a human face, so human, in fact, that it must be seen as the expression of the human striving for power.

15 Ibid., p. 45.

16 Ibid., p. 47.

17 Ibid., p. 45.

18 Ibid., p. 49.

19 Ibid., p. 36.

20 Ibid., pp. 38f.

21 Foucault also ties the formation of public opinion to the written word. See Foucault, *Discipline and Punish*, pp. 95f.: 'These laws must be published, so that everyone has access to them; what is needed is not oral traditions and customs, but a written legislation which can be "the stable monument of the social pact", printed texts available to all: "Only printing can make the public as a whole and not just a few persons depositories of the sacred code of the laws".' [Transl. note: The quotation within the quotation is from de Beccaria, *Traité des délits et des peines*, p. 26].

22 In his historiography of the occident, Giorgio Agamben also gets to grips with the exception, and he turns it into the rule. Thus, the concentration camp becomes the '"nomos" of the modern' (*Homo Sacer*, p. 166). Just as the space of power cannot be explained in terms of the antechamber of power, the political space of the modern cannot be derived from the camp. If one were to look at the *normal cases* of the history of humankind, one would be entitled to cherish the hope that

the *coming human being* will not bear the name *homo sacer* but *homo liber*.

23 Hegel, *Enzyklopädie der philosophischen Wissenschaften III*, p. 221.

24 Arendt, *On Violence*, p. 53. [Transl. note: The passage runs: 'Violence can always destroy power; out of the barrel of a gun grows the most effective command, resulting in the most instant and perfect obedience. What can never grow out of it is power.']

25 The young Nietzsche misunderstands the nature of power when he writes: 'Violence provides the first right, and it does not provide any right that is not founded on acts of arrogation, usurpation, violence.' Nietzsche, *Nachgelassene Schriften 1870–1873*, KSA 1, p. 770.

26 Arendt, *On Violence*, p. 52.

27 Arendt, *The Human Condition*, p. 198.

28 Ibid., p. 199.

29 Ibid., pp. 198f.

30 Ibid., p. 200.

31 Ibid., pp. 204f. (transl. mod.). [Transl. note: The German text includes the clause 'weil sie dem Erscheinen und dem Scheinen selbst dient', which is not part of the English text.]

32 Transl. note: This phrase is again part of an addition to the German version of the text: 'It is like a feeble echo of the pre-philosophical Greek experience of action and speech as sheer actuality [appearing in the brightness of the public created by power, an experience in which action and speech belonged together like the visible and its shadow], to read time and again in political philosophy since Democritus and Plato that politics is a *techne*' (ibid., p. 207).

33 [Transl. note: Another addition to the German text. The terms 'Wirklichkeitsgefühl' and 'Lebensgefühl' have no equivalent in the English text, but see p. 199.] According to Arendt, Hegel's slave, who evades the struggle for power because of a

fear of death, i.e. out of an interest in bare life, cannot achieve a 'sense of reality'. He prefers the 'sense of life'. The master, by contrast, for whom power is more important than merely living, exposes him- or herself to the danger of death, risks his or her life. The battle for power and recognition opens up the 'space of appearance' in which human beings are not just present like things but explicitly appear to each other. For Arendt, this is the point where politics begins. The reality of the political is founded not by the fear of death but by the freedom towards death.

34 Habermas, 'Hannah Arendt: On the Concept of Power', p. 172.

35 Ibid., p. 177. [Transl. note: 'no one really possesses power' appears as Habermas's voice in the translation but is in fact Arendt's, as again the German text diverges from the English.]

36 Arendt, *On Violence*, p. 42.

37 Habermas, 'Hannah Arendt', p. 177. The passage quoted by Habermas is only part of the German *Vita Activa*, not of *The Human Condition*.

38 Arendt, *The Human Condition*, p. 200.

39 Arendt, *On Violence*, p. 50.

40 Long before Arendt, Paul Tillich put forward the thesis that power is based on a collective design for action. See Tillich, *The Socialist Decision*, p. 138: 'In what is such a capability [of power to prevail], such a fixed possibility, grounded? What is the underlying basis of power? The possibility of social power is based in the necessity of creating a unified social will. A unified will, however, comes to expression only through a leading group, or through an individual designated by the group, in whom this unity is represented and through whom it is expressed. *Thus power is the actualization of social unity.*' Hobbes was also aware of the strength of collective power. See his *Leviathan*, p. 58: 'The greatest of human powers, is that which is compounded of the power of most men, united

by consent, in one person, natural or civil, that has the use of all their powers depending on his will; such as is the power of a commonwealth: or depending on the wills of each particular; such as is the power of a faction or of divers factions leagued.'

41 Habermas, 'Hannah Arendt', p. 173.

42 Arendt, *On Violence*, p. 51. [Transl. note: The sentence in square brackets is not part of the English text.] This passage again illustrates that Arendt's reflections lack argumentative rigour. Arendt often shifts the level of argument arbitrarily or on the basis of associations. These shifts produce a conceptual vagueness.

43 Habermas, 'Hannah Arendt', pp. 179f.

44 Honneth perceives power only from the perspective of domination or social struggle. He therefore misses the dimension of power in which it is constitutive. See Honneth, *The Critique of Power*.

45 Arendt, *The Human Condition*, p. 201.

46 Habermas, 'Hannah Arendt', p. 184.

47 Ibid., p. 183.

48 Ibid., p. 181. On the abstract notion of consensus, any deviation from it appears as violence. As early as the 1970s, Habermas wrote: 'Insofar as norms express generalizable interests, they are based on a rational consensus ... Insofar as norms do not regulate generalizable interests, they are based on force [*Gewalt*] [sic!, B-C. H.]; in the latter context we use the term normative power [*Macht*].' Habermas, *Legitimation Crisis*, p. 111.

49 Habermas, 'Hannah Arendt', p. 184 [italics reinstated].

50 For Habermas, any attempt by the political leadership to create spaces for decisions, and thus to create power, can only be suspicious. Approving of a point made by Arendt, he writes: 'From the perspective of systems theory, the generation of power appears as a problem that can be solved by the political leadership's having a stronger influence on the will of

the populace. In the measure that this occurs by the means of psychic compulsion, with persuasion and manipulation, it is in Arendt's terms a matter of an increase in violence but not of a growth in the power of the political system, for according to her hypothesis power can arise only within structures of communication free from compulsion; it cannot be generated "from above".' Ibid., p. 182.

5 The Ethics of Power

1 Schmitt, *The Nomos of the Earth in the International Law of the Jus Publicum Europaeum*, p. 49.
2 Ibid., p. 47.
3 Ibid., p. 48.
4 Ibid., p. 47. [Transl. note: The German term 'Ortung' expresses both the identification of a place (when read as a verbal noun derived from 'orten' – 'to locate') and the transformation of a neutral ground into an identifiable place (when read as a noun-based phrase derived from 'Ort' ('place')). The English translation as 'orientation' aims to capture some of both these senses. Note that 'Ort' in Heidegger is translated as 'site'; thus, the semantic connection between Schmitt and Heidegger which Han establishes is masked.]
5 Heidegger, 'Language in the Poem: A Discussion on Georg Trakl's Poetic Work', p. 159. [Transl. note: The English translation omits Heidegger's reference to the tip of a spear as the referent of the name 'Ort': 'Ursprünglich bedeutet der Name 'Ort' die Spitze des Speers.']
6 Heidegger, 'Letter on Humanism', p. 274.
7 Heidegger, 'Language in the Poem', p. 160.
8 Ibid.
9 Transl. note: See note 5.
10 Although Heidegger's aim is to interrogate power 'metaphysically with regard to its essence', he only perceives power in its negative form as 'machination', without crediting it with

any positivity (*The History of Beyng*, p. 57). Thus, it becomes juxtaposed to 'that which is in no need of power' (ibid., p. 60). The '*nomos*' that is not 'fabricated by human reason' yet guarantees 'the experience of something that we can hold on to' would offer 'a hold for all conduct' ('Letter on Humanism', p. 274), accordingly it would not require any power. Thus, Heidegger does not see the connection between gathering, *logos* and power.

11 Heidegger, 'Language in the Poem', pp. 159f.

12 Derrida, *Rogues*, p. 17.

13 Beck, *Power in the Global Age*, p. 57.

14 See ibid., p. 52: 'It is the world of business in particular that has developed such meta-power by breaking out of the cage of the territorial nation-state-organized power game and mastering new strategies of power in the digital domain in contrast to territorially rooted states.'

15 The global market *as such* is not a power structure, not even a diffuse one. It is dispersed into a large number of economic and political power structures, which makes the formation of an overarching power structure impossible. An *altogether diffuse* power is no power at all because total dispersion means that any kind of ipsocentric intentionality, which is necessary for the establishment of power, disappears. Beck, however, hypostasizes the global economy into a 'diffuse power, *diffuse* because', he argues, 'it is anonymous and lacks a centre, attributability and clear structures of responsibility' (ibid., p. 56). A transnational corporation, by contrast, is a power structure. Its decentralized organization does not imply structural diffusion. Rather, it represents a strategic dispersion. A decentralized organization may even generate more power than one that is centralized.

16 Transl. note: The German neologism 'Ab-Ort' plays on 'abseits gelegen' ('remote') and 'Abort' ('lavatory', but also 'abortion').

17 It is mainly totalitarian sites that produce the off-sites that are not allowed to present themselves as sites and that are not acknowledged as parts of a site. Thus, 'camps' are off-sites. But when Agamben assigns to the 'camp' the status of being the 'hidden matrix of the politics in which we are still living' (*Homo Sacer*, p. 175), he thereby declares it to be the foundation of the site. A site *may be able* to produce an off-site, but it is not *based* on it. A site with a high level of mediation does not have *de-siting [entortend]* effects. Likewise, *homo liber*, which is perhaps the human being to come, does not necessarily presuppose *homo sacer*, who is the inmate without the rights of an off-site. Nevertheless, the possibility of off-sites again gives rise to the question of the *ethical dimension of sites*, i.e. of power.

18 Derrida, *Rogues*, p. 150.

19 Ibid., p. 148.

20 Capital, like cape, captain, or capitol, is derived from Latin *caput*, meaning 'tip' or 'head'.

21 Foucault, 'The Ethics of the Concern for Self as a Practice of Freedom', p. 292. We should note, however, that Foucault's analyses of power are largely dominated by the model of struggle-repression: 'It is obvious that all my work in recent years has been couched in the schema of struggle-repression, and it is this – which I have hitherto been attempting to apply – which I have now been forced to reconsider, both because it is still insufficiently elaborated at a whole number of points, and because I believe that these two notions of repression and war must themselves be considerably modified if not ultimately abandoned. In any case, I believe that they must be submitted to closer scrutiny ... The need to investigate this notion of repression more thoroughly springs therefore from the impression I have that it is wholly inadequate to the analysis of the mechanisms and effects of power that it is so pervasively used to characterise today' (Foucault, 'Two Lectures' [Lecture of 7 January 1976], p. 92).

22 Foucault, 'The Subject and Power', p. 790

23 See ibid., p. 789: 'A relationship of violence acts upon a body or upon things; it forces, it bends, it breaks on the wheel, it destroys, or it closes the door on all possibilities. Its opposite pole can only be passivity, and if it comes up against any resistance, it has no other option but to try to minimize it. On the other hand, a power relationship can only be articulated on the basis of two elements which are each indispensable if it is really to be a power relationship: that "the other" (the one over whom power is exercised) be thoroughly recognized and maintained to the very end as a person who acts; and that, faced with a relationship of power, a whole field of responses, reactions, results, and possible inventions may open up.'

24 Ibid., p. 794. [Transl. note: The part in square brackets – 'ohne eventuelle Umkehrung' – is not part of the English text.]

25 Foucault, 'The Ethics of the Concern for Self as a Practice of Freedom', p. 298.

26 Ibid., p. 299.

27 Ibid., p. 298.

28 Ibid., p. 283.

29 Ibid.

30 Ibid., p. 284.

31 Foucault, *The Hermeneutics of the Subject*, p. 210.

32 Ibid., p. 109.

33 Foucault, 'The Ethics of the Concern for Self as a Practice of Freedom', p. 288.

34 Foucault, *The History of Sexuality, Vol. 2*, p. 79.

35 Foucault, 'The Ethics of the Concern for Self as a Practice of Freedom', p. 288.

36 Foucault, *The History of Sexuality, Vol. 2*, pp. 80f.

37 Transl. note: the expression alludes to a circularity that attaches to economic exchange based on equivalences.

38 Foucault, 'The Ethics of the Concern for Self as a Practice of Freedom', p. 287.

39 By defining power as an attempt to determine the conduct of others – which simply amounts to being with *oneself* in the other, or to returning to *oneself* in the other – Foucault ultimately acknowledges the ipsocentric character of power.

40 Foucault, *The Hermeneutics of the Subject*, p. 251.

41 Nietzsche, *Beyond Good and Evil*, p. 153.

42 Ibid. (transl. mod.).

43 Ibid.

44 Ibid.

45 Nietzsche, *Nachgelassene Fragmente 1880–1882*, KSA 9, p. 550.

46 Nietzsche, *Nachgelassene Fragmente 1887–1889*, KSA 13, p. 360.

47 Nietzsche, *Nachgelassene Fragmente 1884–1885*, KSA 11, p. 700.

48 Ibid.

49 Nietzsche, *Nachgelassene Fragmente 1885–1887*, KSA 12, p. 290.

50 Nietzsche, *Nachgelassene Fragmente 1884–1885*, KSA 11, p. 188.

51 Nietzsche, *On the Genealogy of Morality*, p. 49.

52 Nietzsche, *Human, All-Too Human*, p. 202.

53 Nietzsche, *Nachgelassene Fragmente 1880–1882*, KSA 9, p. 211.

54 Nietzsche, *Human, All-Too Human*, p. 202.

55 Ibid.

56 Nietzsche, *Daybreak*, p. 209.

57 Nietzsche, *Nachgelassene Fragmente 1882–1884*, KSA 10, p. 88.

58 Nietzsche, *Daybreak*, p. 196.

59 This aristocratic friendliness does not indiscriminately welcome everything. See Nietzsche, *Nachgelassene Fragmente 1887–1889*, KSA 13, p. 9: 'Making do with people and making one's heart an open house: that is liberal but not noble. You can recognize those hearts that are capable of noble hospital-

ity by the many draped windows and closed shutters: they keep their *best* rooms at the very least *empty*; they expect guests with whom one does *not* have to make do....'

60 Nietzsche, *Nachgelassene Fragmente 1885–1887*, KSA 12, p. 67.

61 See Aristotle, *Nicomachean Ethics*, p. 170 [1166a].

62 Boundless friendliness must also be opposed to communicative friendliness based on the principle of exchange, because friendliness as a communicative 'technique' is the 'ability' to 'delay the expression of one's own opinions and expectations until the right moment has come'. The waiting period is 'usefully filled with reacting to the representations of the other'. Communicative friendliness is guided by the 'principle of the correct temporal placement of one's own expectations and simultaneous consideration for the self-presentation of the other'. In terms of systems theory, it serves the purpose of the 'elastic adaptation of formal systems to their environment' (Luhmann, *Funktionen und Folgen formaler Organisation*, pp. 361f.). A 'system' is 'friendly' if it helps another to cut a *good figure*, i.e. to produce a successful self-presentation. A 'friendly person' should treat the other 'the way the other wants to appear'. As 'tact', friendliness is a 'behaviour with which A presents himself as the one whom B needs as a partner, to be able to be the one that he would like to present in A's eyes' (Luhmann, *A Sociological Theory of Law*, p. 27). Thus, communicative friendliness as a *technique* does not possess an asymmetrical structure. The friendly person is *eyeing* the right moment for launching his or her own expectations or opinions, i.e. *him- or herself*, on the communicative field of exchanges. In this context, passive or active listening, which helps the other achieve a successful self-presentation, is put up with as a detour on the way to reaching one's own self-presentation. Thus, communicative friendliness is an act of exchange informed by care of the self.

63 Nietzsche, *Beyond Good and Evil*, p. 154.

64 Ibid.

65 Nietzsche, *Nachgelassene Fragmente 1882–1884*, KSA 10, p. 508.

66 Nietzsche, *Thus Spoke Zarathustra*, p. 162.

67 Nietzsche, *Daybreak*, p. 158. Hobbes, too, explains generosity in economic terms: 'Also riches joined with liberality, is power; because it procureth friends, and servants: without liberality, not so; because in this case they defend not; but expose men to envy, as a prey.' *Leviathan*, p. 58.

68 Nietzsche, letter to F. Rhode (7 October 1869), *Briefwechsel: Kritische Gesamtausgabe*, pp. 61–2.

69 Without a *name*, power cannot form. 'God' is *The name as such*. *No one* has no power. Power is a *phenomenon belonging to someone*. See Nietzsche, *Daybreak*, p. 194: 'It is so unmagnanimous always to play the bestower and giver and to show one's face when doing so! But to give and bestow and to conceal one's name and awareness one is bestowing a favour! Or *to have no name*, like nature, in which the most refreshing thing of all is that here we at last no longer encounter a giver and bestower, a "gracious countenance"! – To be sure, you have frivolously sacrificed even this refreshment, for you have put a god into nature – and now everything is again tense and unfree!' (emph. B.-Ch. H.).

70 The ethics of a friendliness free of intentions knows that *naturalness*, that *silence* or *no oneness [Niemandigkeit]*, in which a fruit falls, 'content and unawares', happy, as opposed to the ethics of Levinas, whose emphatic 'for-the-other' breaks any *silence*.

71 Nietzsche, 'Dionysus Dithyrambs', p. 313.

BIBLIOGRAPHY

Agamben, Giorgio, *Homo Sacer: Sovereign Power and Bare Life*, trans. Daniel Heller-Roazen, Stanford, 1998.

Arendt, Hannah, *On Violence*, New York, 1970.

— *The Human Condition*, Chicago, 1998.

Aristotle, *Nicomachean Ethics*, trans. Terence H. Irwin, Cambridge, 2000.

Bachrach, Peter and Morton S. Baratz, 'Two Faces of Power', *The American Political Science Review* 56 (1962), pp. 947–52.

Bataille, Georges, *Theory of Religion*, trans. Robert Hurley, New York, 1989.

— *Theorie der Religion*, ed. with an afterword by Gerd Bergfleth, Berlin, 1997.

de Beccaria, C. *Traité des délits et des peines*, trans. André Morellet, Paris, 1764, ed. 1856.

Beck, Ulrich, *Power in the Global Age*, trans. Kathleen Cross, Cambridge, 2005.

Berle, Adolf A., *Macht: Die treibende Kraft der Geschichte*, Hamburg, 1973.

Bourdieu, Pierre, *Distinction: A Social Critique of the Judgment of Taste*, trans. Richard Nice, London, 1984.

— *Satz und Gegensatz: Über die Verantwortung des Intellektuellen*, Berlin, 1989.

— *The Logic of Practice*, trans. Richard Nice, Cambridge, 1990.

— *The Political Ontology of Martin Heidegger*, trans. Peter Collier, Cambridge, 1991.

— 'Die männliche Herrschaft', in Irene Dölling and Beate Krais (eds), *Ein alltägliches Spiel: Geschlechterkonstruktion in der sozialen Praxis*, Frankfurt/M., 1997, pp. 153–217.

— 'Eine sanfte Gewalt: Pierre Bourdieu im Gespräch mit Irene Dölling und Margarete Steinrück', in Irene Dölling and Beate Krais (eds), *Ein alltägliches Spiel: Geschlechterkonstruktion in der sozialen Praxis*, Frankfurt/M., 1997, pp. 218–230.

Burckhardt, Jacob, *Reflections on History*, trans. M. D. Hottinger, Indianapolis, 1979.

Butler, Judith, *The Psychic Life of Power: Theories in Subjection*, Stanford, 1997.

Canetti, Elias, *Crowds and Power*, New York, 1973 [1960].

Dean, Mitchell, *Governmentality: Power and Rule in Modern Society*, London, 2001.

Derrida, Jacques, *Rogues: Two Essays on Reason*, trans. Pascale-Anne Brault and Michael Naas, Stanford, 2005.

Fink-Eitel, Hinrich, *Foucault zur Einführung*, Hamburg, 1989.

Foucault, Michel, *Mikrophysik der Macht: Über Strafjustiz, Psychiatrie und Medizin*, Berlin, 1976.

— *Dispositive der Macht: Über Sexualität, Wissen und Wahrheit*, Berlin, 1978.

— *History of Sexuality, Vol. 1: The Will to Knowledge*, trans. Robert Hurley, New York, 1978.

— 'Power and Norm: Notes', in M. Morris and P. Patton

(eds), *Michel Foucault: Power, Truth, Strategy*, Sydney, 1978, pp. 59–66.

— 'The History of Sexuality', in Colin Gordon (ed.), *Power/ Knowledge: Selected Interviews and Other Writings 1972– 1977*, New York, 1980.

— 'Two Lectures' [Lecture of 7 January 1976], in Colin Gordon (ed.), *Power/Knowledge: Selected Interviews and Other Writings 1972–1977*, New York, 1980.

— 'The Subject and Power', *Critical Inquiry* 8:4 (Summer 1982), pp. 777–95.

— 'Truth and Power', in Paul Rabinow (ed.), *The Foucault Reader*, New York, 1984, pp. 51–75.

— *Freiheit und Selbstsorge: Interview 1984 und Vorlesung 1982*, Frankfurt/M., 1985.

— *The History of Sexuality, Vol. 2: The Use of Pleasure*, New York, 1990.

— *Discipline and Punish: The Birth of the Prison*, trans. Alan Sheridan, New York, 1995.

— 'The Ethics of the Concern for Self as a Practice of Freedom', in Paul Rabinow (ed.), *Ethics: Subjectivity and Truth*, New York, 1997, pp. 281–301.

— *Society Must be Defended*, trans. David Macey, London, 2003.

— *The Hermeneutics of the Subject*, trans. Graham Burchell, New York, 2005.

French, Marilyn, *Beyond Power: On Women, Man and Morals*, New York, 1985.

Göhler, Gerhard (ed.), *Macht der Öffentlichkeit – Öffentlichkeit der Macht*, Baden-Baden, 1995.

— et al., *Institution – Macht – Repräsentation: Wofür politische Institutionen stehen und wie sie wirken*, Baden-Baden, 1997.

Greven, Michael Th. (ed.), *Macht in der Demokratie: Denkanstöße zur Wiederbelebung einer klassischen Frage in der zeitgenössischen Politischen Theorie*, Baden-Baden, 1991.

Habermas, Jürgen, *Legitimation Crisis*, trans. Thomas McCarthy, Cambridge, 1988.

— 'Hannah Arendt: On the Concept of Power', in *Philosophical-Political Profiles*, trans. Frederick G. Lawrence, Cambridge, 2012, pp. 171–87.

Han, Byung-Chul, *Todesarten*, Munich, 1998.

— *Philosophie des Zen-Buddhismus*, Stuttgart, 2002.

— *Tod und Alterität*, Munich, 2002.

Handke, Peter, 'Essay on Tiredness', in *The Jukebox and Other Essays on Storytelling*, New York, 1994.

Hegel, Georg Wilhelm Friedrich, *Vorlesungen über die Philosophie der Religion I*, Frankfurt/M., 1969.

— *Vorlesungen über die Philosophie der Religion II*, Frankfurt/M., 1969.

— *Berliner Schriften 1822–1831*, Frankfurt/M., 1970.

— *Enzyklopädie der philosophischen Wissenschaften III*, Frankfurt/M., 1970.

— *Enzyklopädie der philosophischen Wissenschaften: Dritter Teil: Die Philosophie des Geistes mit den mündlichen Zusätzen*, Frankfurt/M., 1970.

— *Werke in zwanzig Bänden*, Frankfurt/M., 1970.

— *Aesthetics: Lectures on Fine Art, Vol. I*, trans. T. M. Knox, Oxford, 1975.

— *The Phenomenology of Spirit*, trans. A. V. Miller, Oxford, 1977.

— *Elements of the Philosophy of Right*, trans. H. B. Nisbet, Cambridge, 1991.

— *Hegel's Philosophy of Nature: Part Two of the Encyclopedia of the Philosophical Sciences (1830)*, trans. A. V. Miller, Oxford, 2004.

— *Encyclopedia of the Philosophical Sciences in Outline, Part I: Science of Logic*, trans. Klaus Brinkmann and Daniel O. Dahlstrom, Cambridge, 2010.

— *The Science of Logic II*, trans. George di Giovanni,

Cambridge, 2010.

— *Lectures on the Philosophy of History*, trans. Ruben Alvarado, Aalten, 2011.

Heidegger, Martin, *Being and Time*, trans. John Macquarrie and Edward Robinson, Oxford, 1962.

— 'Language in the Poem: A Discussion on Georg Trakl's Poetic Work', in *On the Way to Language*, trans. Peter D. Hertz, New York, 1971.

— *Gesamtausgabe*, Frankfurt/M., 1975ff.

— *The Will to Power as Art, Vols I and II*, trans. David Farrell Krell, New York, 1991.

— 'Letter on Humanism', trans. Frank A. Capuzzi, in *Pathmarks*, Cambridge, 1998, pp. 239–76.

— *Pathmarks*, ed. William McNeill, Cambridge, 1998.

— *The History of Beyng*, trans. William McNeill and Jeffrey Powell, Bloomington, IN, 2015.

Hindess, Barry, *Discourses of Power: From Hobbes to Foucault*, Oxford, 1996.

Hobbes, Thomas, *Leviathan*, Oxford, 2008 [1651].

Hondrich, Karl Otto, *Theorie der Herrschaft*, Frankfurt/M., 1973.

Honneth, Axel, *The Critique of Power: Reflective Stages in a Critical Social Theory*, trans. Kenneth Baynes, Cambridge MA, 1991.

Imbusch, Peter (ed.), *Macht und Herrschaft: Sozialwissenschaftliche Konzeptionen und Theorien*, Opladen, 1998.

Kantorowicz, Ernst, *The King's Two Bodies: A Study in Medieval Political Theology*, Princeton, 1957.

Kelly, Michael (ed.), *Critique and Power: Recasting the Foucault/Habermas Debate*, Cambridge MA, 1994.

Kneer, Georg, *Rationalisierung, Disziplinierung und Differenzierung: Sozialtheorie und Zeitdiagnose bei Habermas, Foucault und Luhmann*, Opladen, 1996.

127

Lemke, Thomas, *Eine Kritik der politischen Vernunft: Foucaults Analyse der modernen Gouvernementalität*, Berlin and Hamburg, 1997.

Levinas, Emmanuel, *Otherwise than Being, or, Beyond Essence*, trans. Alphonso Lingis, Dordrecht, 1991.

Likert, Rensis, *Neue Ansätze der Unternehmensführung*, Bern and Stuttgart, 1972.

Luhmann, Niklas, 'Klassische Theorie der Macht: Kritik ihrer Prämissen', *Zeitschrift für Politik* 2 (1969), pp. 149–70.

— 'Macht und System. Ansätze zur Analyse von Macht in der Politikwissenschaft', *Universitas: Zeitschrift für Wissenschaft, Kunst und Literatur* 5 (1977), pp. 473–82.

— *Soziologische Aufklärung 1: Aufsätze zur Theorie sozialer Systeme*, Opladen, 1984.

— *Soziologische Aufklärung 4: Beiträge zur funktionalen Differenzierung der Gesellschaft*, Opladen, 1987.

— *Funktionen und Folgen formaler Organisation*, Berlin, 1995.

— *A Sociological Theory of Law*, trans. Elizabeth King-Utz and Martin Albrow, London, 2014.

— 'Power', in *Trust and Power*, ed. Christian Morgner and Michael King, Cambridge, 2017.

Machiavelli, Niccolo, *The Prince*, London, 2009.

Mann, Michael, *The Sources of Social Power: History of Power From the Beginning to AD 1760*, Vol. 1, Cambridge, 1986.

Miller, Peter, *Domination and Power*, London and New York, 1987.

Morgan, Ivor, *Power and Politics*, London, 1999.

Morris, Peter, *Power: A Philosophical Analysis*, Manchester, 1987.

Nietzsche, Friedrich, *Briefwechsel*, in *Kritische Gesamtausgabe*, Vol. 2, 1, Berlin, 1977.

— *Human, All-Too Human*, trans. R. J. Hollingdale, Cambridge, 1986.

— *Sämtliche Werke. Kritische Studienausgabe*, 15 vols, Munich, Berlin and New York, 1988.

— *Daybreak*, trans. R. J. Hollingdale, Cambridge, 1997.

— *Beyond Good and Evil*, trans. Judith Norman, Cambridge, 2002.

— *Twilight of the Idols, or How to Philosophize with a Hammer*, in *The Anti-Christ, Ecce Homo, Twilight of the Idols, and Other Writings*, trans. Judith Norman, Cambridge, 2005.

— *Thus Spoke Zarathustra*, trans. Adrian Del Caro, Cambridge, 2006.

— *On the Genealogy of Morality*, trans. Carol Diethe, Cambridge, 2007.

— 'Dionysus Dithyrambs', in *The Peacock and the Buffalo: The Poetry of Nietzsche*, trans. James Luchte, London, 2010.

Parsons, Talcott, 'On the Concept of Political Power', *Proceedings of the American Philosophical Society* 107:3 (1963), pp. 232–62.

— *Politics and Social Structure*, New York and London, 1969.

Plessner, Helmuth, *Macht und menschliche Natur*, in *Gesammelte Schriften*, Vol. 5, Frankfurt/M., 1981.

Popitz, Heinrich, *Phänomene der Macht: Autorität, Herrschaft, Gewalt, Technik*, Tübingen, 1986.

Ptassek, Peter et al., *Macht und Meinung: Die rhetorische Konstitution der politischen Welt*, Göttingen, 1992.

Röttgers, Kurt, *Spuren der Macht*, Freiburg and Munich, 1990.

Russell, Bertrand, *Power*, London, 2004 [1938].

Carl Schmitt, *Political Theology*, trans. George Schwab, Cambridge MA, 1985.

— *The Nomos of the Earth in the International Law of the Jus Publicum Europaeum*, trans. G. L. Ulmen, New York, 2003.

— *Dialogues on Power and Space*, trans. Samuel Garrett Zeitlin, Cambridge, 2015.

Sofsky, Wolfgang, *Traktat über die Gewalt*, Frankfurt/M., 1996.

— *The Order of Terror: The Concentration Camp*, Princeton, 1997.

— and Reiner Paris, *Figurationen sozialer Macht: Autorität – Stellvertretung – Koalition*, Frankfurt/M., 1994.

Tillich, Paul, *Love, Power, and Justice: Ontological Analyses and Ethical Applications*, Oxford, 1954.

— 'Das Problem der Macht: Versuch einer philosophischen Grundlegung', in *Gesammelte Werke*, Vol. 2, ed. Renate Albrecht, Stuttgart, 1962, pp. 193–208.

— 'Philosophie der Macht', in *Gesammelte Werke*, Vol. 9, Stuttgart, 1967, pp. 205–32.

— *The Socialist Decision*, trans. Franklin Sherman, Eugene, 2012.

Weber, Max, *Economy and Society: An Outline of Interpretive Sociology*, Berkeley and Los Angeles, 1978.

Zenkert, Georg, 'Hegel und das Problem der Macht', *Deutsche Zeitschrift für Philosophie* 43 (1995), pp. 435–51.